Beyond Hands-On

Techniques for Using Color, Scent, Taste, Touch and Sound to Enhance Learning

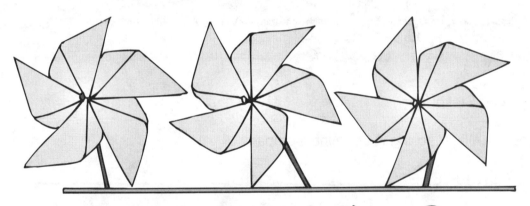

Written by Dr. Linda Karges-Bone
Illustrated by Luda Stekol

Teaching & Learning Company
1204 Buchanan St., P.O. Box 10
Carthage, IL 62321

This book belongs to

_____

Cover by Luda Stekol

Copyright © 1996, Teaching & Learning Company

ISBN No. 1-57310-067-6

Printing No. 987654321

Teaching & Learning Company
1204 Buchanan St., P.O. Box 10
Carthage, IL 62321

TLC10067 Copyright © Teaching & Learning Company, Carthage, IL 62321

Dedication

This book is dedicated to the children of Camp Joy and especially to a little boy named Louis Brown, who taught me about being a teacher and a servant. "For with God nothing shall be impossible." Luke 1:37

Acknowledgements

Special thanks to Judy Mitchell and the editorial staff at the Teaching & Learning Company, for believing in the power of innovative thought; to Dr. Robert Rohm of Personality Insights, Atlanta, Georgia; to Professor Myra Jordan of Charleston Southern University, for her insights to music therapy; to Dr. Howard Gardner, whose work has been an inspiration to me for over a decade; to Lisa Quick, for her spiritual support and to the research librarians at Charleston Southern University, for making a writer's work so much more productive.

Table of Contents

Dear Teacher or Parent,

As I was passing around a basket of peppermints, to help my college students focus on their pop quiz, one young fellow (perhaps stalling for time) piped up, "Dr. Bone, I hope these peppermints work. But I'm curious, where did you *find* all this stuff about colors and tastes?"

That's a valid question. Not surprisingly, the answer involves another question. "How can we use our brains better?" While completing my dissertation research on assessment, I began to learn more about the rapidly expanding field of cognitive science. Metacognition. Thinking about thinking. I became curious about how we as teachers and parents, could help children to become more active, critical, involved learners . . . in short, better thinkers.

Many of the answers seem to lie, not in neurology, but in botany, art, music, design, psychology and alternative medicine.

Everyone, it seems, is tapping into the brain's potential, except teachers. We talk about "hands-on" instruction; yet we do not study the differences between left brain and right brain characteristics. We take courses on "learning styles"; yet we never investigate the neurological or sensory basis that underpin the theory. Too often, teachers want only the message and ignore the messenger. In this case, the messenger is the human brain.

The brain reacts to colors, scents, tastes, textures and sounds. Artists know this instinctively. Medical doctors and healers harness the knowledge to keep us healthy or to fight disease. Designers soothe or excite us by manipulating the environment. Marketing specialists influence our buying habits by learning these secrets. And yet, who needs this information more than teachers? Our job description typically defies standard definitions, but who are we if not artists, healers, designers and marketing specialists? In classrooms, through curriculum, with instruction, around assessment and for children, teachers practice all of the skills that I listed. Moreover, we often do so under stress and without support. For ourselves and for the children, we need to learn as much as we can about the brain and how learning can be enhanced. As a former teacher of developmentally challenged children, learning disabled children, "regular" kindergarten children and middle grades gifted learners, I have had plenty of opportunities to think about these concerns.

Keep in mind, however, the techniques outlined in this book have not been "proven" to cause or institute a permanent learning or behavioral change in children. Moreover, these techniques are not intended to replace professional medical or psychological care of children, in the event that such is needed. Instead, psychological research; marketing; sociology; art; music therapy; and learning theory have been applied to the unique art of teaching. The purpose of this book is to share innovative research with teachers, in an attempt to make our work more productive and vital.

The young man who asked me about the peppermints did not do well on the quiz. He told me later that he had not "cracked the book" at all. No amount of peppermint or wintergreen or manipulation of the environment can compensate for a lack of basic knowledge. Yet, most of the students did well, very well.

Perhaps your classroom and your students could benefit from some of these innovations. A child who is hard to reach; a class that is difficult to control; a lack of energy and excitement on your part . . . this book may offer what you need. Enjoy *Beyond Hands-On: Techniques for Using Color, Scent, Taste, Touch and Sound to Enhance Learning*. Let me know what works for you. I plan to do some follow-up research. Right now, however, I need to help my eight-year-old daughter study her multiplication tables. We'll be using mint and scented markers to help her focus. How about you?

In the spring of 1996, I had the enlightening experience of reading Dr. Robert Sylwester's book, *A Celebration of Neurons* (See bibliography). In this exciting text, Dr. Sylwester synthesizes the latest research on cognitive science and suggests applications for curriculum and instruction. To me, endeavoring to use color, scent, taste, texture and music in innovative ways, his discussion of Dr. Gerald Edelman's model of the "brain as a jungle," made perfect sense. (See bibliography.)

According to Dr. Edelman (and what seems to be emerging from the latest in brain imaging) the human brain is not a neatly compartmentalized computer. Instead, it is a "rich, layered, messy, unplanned jungle ecosystem" (Sylwester, 1995).

Draw on your long-term memory and personal sensory experiences, and imagine a jungle: hot colorful, filled with pungent fragrances, a cacophony of sounds and a tapestry of textures. Now, contrast that image with a typical classroom: cool, sterile, abstract. It just doesn't fit!

If the "jungle" model holds true, even in the broadest sense then teachers need to put on safari gear and trek in with the same courageous spirit as explorers. Perhaps, the brain is truly our latest frontier. Perhaps, our students' brains will respond to the richer colors, scents, tastes, textures and music of a classroom safari.

Although the jungle model is intriguing for teachers and researchers, it is perhaps as fraught with peril as a real jungle. With over 100 trillion circuits, the human brain is enormously complicated. Moreover, the delicate balance between genetic wiring and environmental connections makes it a hazardous jungle to travel. In what may be the most reproduced *Newsweek* article to date, author Sharon Begley presents some of the latest research on brain science, as it applies to parenting and teaching very young children. (See bibliography.)

If this research holds true, then parents and teachers must take advantage of very *early* "windows of opportunity" to turn children on to language, mathematics and music. However, as you consider the techniques offered in this book, try on this metaphor. Instead of "Windows of Opportunity" that might quickly and firmly *close*, think instead of a "venting system" flowing continuously into the child's mind. True, there are places and times in which the vents are more open or clear, but if we have hope in the plasticity and flexibility of neurons, then frequent, rich sensory experiences, *throughout childhood* and into adulthood, can encourage thought and creativity.

Sincerely,

Linda

Linda Karges-Bone, Ed.D.

Albert Einstein once said: "We should take care not to make the intellect our god; it has, of course, powerful muscles, but no personality." This book, *Beyond Hands-On: Techniques for Using Color, Scent, Taste, Touch and Sound to Enhance Learning,* is about making learning, the intellect, more personable, creative and friendly. By capturing the powerful creative energy of color, the influence of texture, the persuasion of scent, the excitement of taste and the appeal of sound, and carefully directing them into our classroom instruction, teachers can make their teaching more effective and the children's learning deeper and more lasting.

Is this another New Age attempt at pseudo-psychology? Is it frivolous? Nonacademic? I think not. Instead, *Beyond Hands-On* takes solid research, new innovations and a taste of creative elixir for excitement and presents teachers with new ways to do what they do best ... teaching children. As a writer, professor and mother, I recognize the importance of keeping fresh ideas flowing, but classroom teachers have precious little time to peruse journals, write letters to faraway "experts" or conduct interviews. So, I take it on myself to find the ideas, verify the information and work with talented illustrators, to create resources for my colleagues—classroom teachers.

The journey to this book began more than two years ago, as I completed a review of the literature on cognitive science ... that is, the study of how the brain works. I became interested in the emerging research which suggests that the brain can process information in areas or lobes that we did not previously recognize as capable of that function. For example, gifted mathematicians may use more of their parietal lobes to solve problems, and if those same gifted mathematicians happen to be females, then they may draw on structures in the brain other than the parietal lobe to solve mathematical tasks. The same goes for reading. Yale researchers found that men use one part of the brain, exclusively, to produce language and to read; while women's brains involve several areas to process words. The brain, it seems, can and does operate in many different ways and under stress, can do even more. Consider the way that stroke patients often make impressive recoveries, by stimulating underused parts of their brains to take on tasks that were once accomplished by other gray matter. Can teachers do more to stimulate the brain? We may have to.

The Medical Connection

Around the same time that I was learning about cognition, a series of articles on an emerging learning disability, SLI, or Specific Language Impairment, caught my attention. Simply put, SLI is a learning disability that occurs in about 80% of children who demonstrate dyslexia or difficulty in learning to read. These youngsters have something in common: frequent, chronic, early ear infections. Medical researchers suspect that these children may have long-term, residual hearing loss which, though slight, could prevent them from quickly and easily learning to read through the typical, auditory-visual cues that teachers provide. However, my premise takes the SLI scenario a step further.

Remember your early childhood development training? Do you recall the term *critical period of language*? This theory, which is held by about half the language experts, contends that there is a period in early childhood, roughly between 12 and 24 months of age, when a child's brain is actually "most ready" to acquire language. I explain it to my student teachers in this way.

The Banana Theory of Language

Let's say that you bought a beautiful, perfectly ripe bunch of bananas. You plan to use the bananas to concoct a fresh fruit salad. But something interferes with your plan; you forget about the fruit salad for several days and when you get around to it, the ripe bananas are mottled and soft. They are no longer the best choice for fruit salad, so you add sugar, eggs, flour, spices and nuts, and create banana bread. It takes a lot more effort to use the bananas when they are not at their peak.

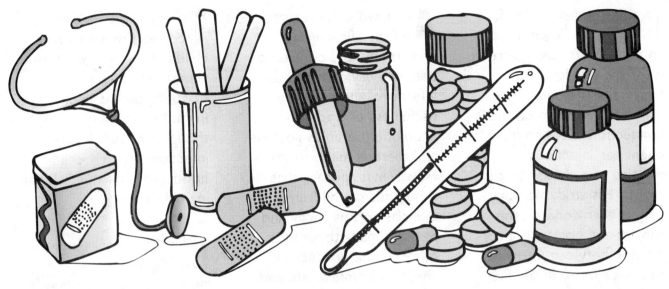

If one believes, even in some small way, the theory of a critical period of language, then chronic early ear infections, especially during the period of 12 to 24 months of age, could interfere with a child's later ability to read. The brain missed an important opportunity. Teachers might want to use creative, multisensory teaching methods to stimulate thinking and learning. In short, SLI could mean more than a residual hearing loss; it could mean a shaky cognitive connection, that might be strengthened by new ways of teaching.

Educators aren't the only ones concerned about chronic early ear infections. Interestingly, financial planners, writing in high stakes money-matters magazines, now direct clients toward investing in companies that do research on creating new antibiotics. It seems that the frequent overprescription of antibiotics for early childhood ear infections has led to the ineffectiveness of once-potent cures such as ampicillin. The bubble gum flavored elixir once cleared up a toddler's earache in a day or so. Today, many antibiotics are no longer effective. This has occurred, in part, because of day care. The typical group day care situation is a breeding ground for colds and ear infections. That is a given.

However, a secondary, more social phenomenon has emerged. Working parents have little choice when it comes to getting back to work. They demand that pediatricians "fix the baby's ear infection" immediately. So many doctors have overprescribed antibiotics for viral infections where they are perhaps not effective. Over time, children, and the bacteria themselves, become immune to antibiotics. Some experts predict that ear infections will become serious early childhood illnesses because our medicines cannot fight the bacteria and because we have not yet developed new infection fighters to take care of the problem.

The Medical Connection

In the summer of 1995, Dr. J. David Osguthorpe, an ear/nose/throat specialist at the Medical University of South Carolina, reported on the connection between frequent ear infections and the size of a child's day care group. His study was the largest ever done on this subject and points to a correlation between frequent (three or more in the first year) ear infections and large day care groups. Clearly, our growing dependence on group day care suggests a growing problem with early childhood ear infections and, perhaps, later learning problems for those same youngsters.

Admittedly, the research on specific language impairment, the connection between day care and ear infections, and even the usefulness of traditional antibiotic therapies goes on and there is much to learn. However, it appears that thousands of children in our classrooms today and perhaps many thousands more, as the product of chronic ear infections, ineffective treatments and resulting specific language impairments, may present new teaching challenges and demand innovative, multisensory instructional techniques such as those outlined in this book.

To make the medical connection to early childhood language intervention clear, Dr. Osguthorpe has been invited to share his thoughts about chronic ear infections in early childhood and subsequent learning delays.

Like the bananas in my metaphor, the time is ripe for introducing new methods into the classroom. In Europe and America, renewed attention has been directed toward what is called *alternative medicine*. In fact, the National Institute of Health recently initiated a new branch, to study the impact and trends in alternative medicine. Over one third of the physicians in America report using "natural" remedies or recommending such practices to their patients, prompting the founding of the Office of the Alternative Medicine (OAM) at the federal level. Furthermore, Dr. Diane Ackerman's book, *A Natural History of the Senses,* ignited interest in the rich, historical base for the use of color, texture, scent and taste in cultures around the globe.

Even so, putting cognitive science, medical science, anthropology, aromatherapy and educational theory aside for a moment, *Beyond Hands-On* is about creative teaching, and—dare I say it?—about having fun in the classroom. When, as a college professor, I provide strong peppermints for my students as they take quizzes or pass out orange highlighting pens for my daughters to use as they prepare for a spelling test, the learning task becomes more fun, and often, more effective.

The five sections in *Beyond Hands-On* offer simple, easily implemented ways of introducing a multi-sensory approach to learning. Students who struggle with language delays, because of chronic early ear infections or other reasons; those who demonstrate Attention Deficit Disorders; those who are easily distracted and those who simply love color, scent and texture . . . all these youngsters, and you as their teacher, will enjoy and hopefully benefit from using all of your senses to learn.

Everyone, it seems, is rethinking the use of sensory experiences. Why not classroom teachers? We already have the blessing of our own experts. Dr. Maria Montessori's sensory-rich methods have guided thousands of early childhood teachers. Dr. Jerome Bruner's efforts to direct teachers toward cognitive science renew curriculum specialists today. Dr. Howard Gardner's pivotal work, *Frame of Mind*, a discussion of the theory of "multiple intelligences," paves the way to use varied techniques to address diverse talents and skills. Finally, my personal favorite, Dr. John Dewey, and his reliance on the power of personal experience to influence learning, leads me to believe that the intense, very intimate experiences of perceiving color, scent, taste, texture and auditory stimulation, as part of an *academic experience*, could be potent and influential.

Chapter 1

Why Move Beyond Hands-On Instruction?

During the past decade, most successful educational theories and practices have centered around a "hands-on" approach to learning. Whether the curriculum dealt with science, mathematics or language, the focus moved to "hands-on," a belief that children of all ages learn best when they are actively involved in learning. The use of manipulatives in mathematics instruction, experiments and samples in science instruction and journal writing in language instruction offer good examples of a hands-on approach to teaching and learning.

math manipulatives

journal writing

science experiments

cooking activities

technology

Research on Left Brain/Right Brain Learning

However in the late 1990s, research in cognitive theory, learning theory and even medicine, suggests a move beyond hands-on to what we might call *minds-on* instruction. How does a primary school teacher move *beyond* hands-on instruction? This book shares specific, easily implemented techniques for the preK to third grade classroom. Yet, to get the full impact of this movement, it helps to look at the curriculum changes which led to this new way of teaching. Research on "left brain/right brain" learning styles influences our teaching today.

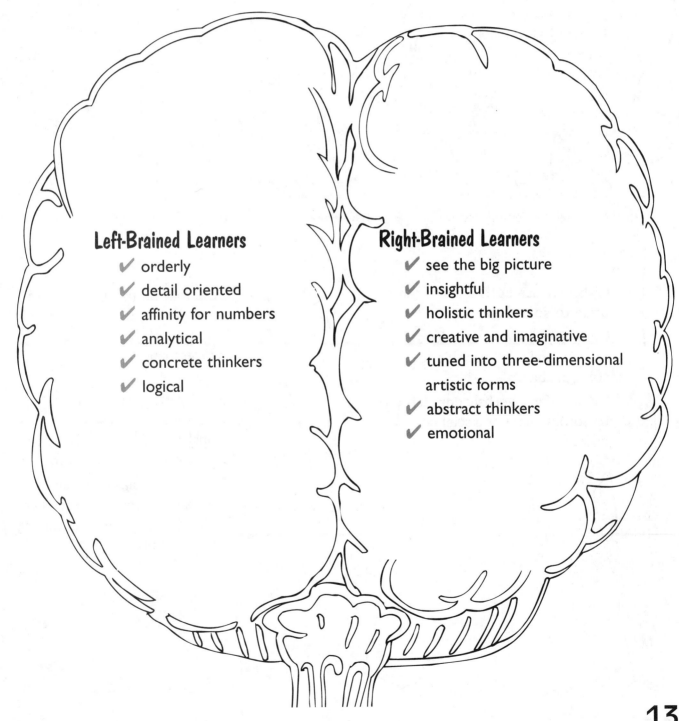

Left-Brained Learners
- ✔ orderly
- ✔ detail oriented
- ✔ affinity for numbers
- ✔ analytical
- ✔ concrete thinkers
- ✔ logical

Right-Brained Learners
- ✔ see the big picture
- ✔ insightful
- ✔ holistic thinkers
- ✔ creative and imaginative
- ✔ tuned into three-dimensional artistic forms
- ✔ abstract thinkers
- ✔ emotional

Research on Left Brain/Right Brain Learning

Although most people use both sides of their brains routinely, we often see children who appear to favor one particular hemisphere. Hands-on techniques, though important, should also be geared to a child's "brain style." In addition to the research on left/right brain learning, other branches of cognitive science suggests "gender differences" related to instruction.

✔ Girls may use both sides of the brain to sound out words.

✔ Girls may draw on emotions more readily and use this to solve problems.

✔ Girls prefer a verbal approach to solving math and science tasks.

✔ Boys may be more subject to dyslexia, because they use only one side of the brain to process language.

✔ Boys may draw on physical activity more readily than emotions. This may often translate into a shorter attention span in the classroom.

✔ Boys may display a literal approach to math and science tasks; doing rather than talking about the process.

14

In addition to investigating the differences between male and female learning characteristics, science and psychology have both turned their attention to the role of "personality" in the human experience. As teachers of young children, we now recognize the importance of "temperament" and acknowledge the fact that children are "born with" a pre-disposition for a certain kind of personality. Dr. Jerome Kagan, a Harvard developmental psychologist, and author of an important book on the biological influence on personality, suggests three distinct personality archetypes:

The Anxious or Inhibited Child

✔ quiet and reflective
✔ intellectual

The Aggressive Child

✔ fearless and often impulsive

The Uninhibited or Bold Child

✔ energetic, yet curious and confident

Temperament/Personality

Most children display "shades of temperament," either in boldness or anxiousness. Fewer children are highly aggressive. However, teachers have a growing body of research to support what they have suspected for a long time: personality has a strong neurochemical base and children display a distinct personality type in infancy. By preschool, a child's personality has a strong influence on the way that parents, siblings and care givers relate to him or her.

While Dr. Kagan's work focuses on a biochemical root of personality, other psychosocial models for personality offer a similar insight. Dr. Robert Rohm, a psychologist who specializes in personality analysis, and who is a former elementary school principal and father of four daughters, suggests four distinct personality types:

The "D" Personality

✔ dominant
✔ demanding
✔ decisive

These children want to be in charge. They enjoy solving problems and taking on tasks but want to be in control of the people involved.

The "I" Personality

✔ impulsive
✔ intuitive

These children prefer people over tasks but want to have fun, make friends and be liked. In the classroom, these children are popular and persuasive. They excel in cooperative groups.

16

Temperament/Personality

Whether one embraces a biological or psychological explanation for personality or a balance between the two, it is clear that personality plays a critical role in how a child learns. Clearly teaching demands more than just content and delivery. It requires insight and sensitivity to personality, gender differences and cognitive learning styles.

The "S" Personality

✔ shy
✔ sweet

These children can be easily swayed. They prefer people over tasks but will work hard to please a teacher or parent. These are the peacemakers in a classroom or work group.

The "C" Personality

✔ cautious
✔ careful

These children may seem cool and difficult, but they prefer to size up a situation before committing. These children prefer tasks over people and may enjoy independent rather than group work.

17

Thinking About Thinking

Teachers in the future will be more concerned with the *metacognition* of teaching. Simply put, *metacognition* means "thinking about thinking." It is not enough to provide hands-on experiences. We have a rich and growing knowledge base about how those experiences should be provided.

These questions can never be answered in the same way in every learning situation. As we learned earlier, important influences such as gender, personality and environment have a powerful influence on each child's life, in and out of the classroom. However, there appears to be a growing body of research, some ancient and some cutting edge, that suggests a role for the senses in primary classrooms. As the title of this book points out, a sensory-rich classroom goes beyond manipulatives and draws on multiple sources of sensation to stimulate thinking, creativity and attention in children.

✔ What colors enhance learning and in what context?

✔ How can scent or the art of aromatherapy work to stimulate the brain?

✔ In what ways might taste, a powerful human motivator, reinforce learning?

✔ When might the sense of touch, especially temperature and texture affect the learning process?

This is a fitting book for our time, since the 1990s have been declared the "Decade of the Brain."

In fact, on July 25, 1989, President George Bush, responding to reports from the National Advisory Councils of the National Institute of Mental Health and the urging of Congress, signed a presidential declaration naming the 1990s as the "Decade of the Brain." The purpose of this effort was to coordinate and support extensive research and study into the functions and organization of the brain and also to find ways to prevent or treat dysfunction in the brain and nervous system. Clearly, the opportunities for enhanced study of the brain have increased significantly, as sophisticated medical imaging techniques such as PET scanning, CAT scanning and MRI scanning (which uses heat, radiation and magnets, in that order) to look inside the brain without surgery, expose new and profound information about the function of this powerful three-pound organ. As teachers of young children, we need to learn as much as possible about brain function and dysfunction, so that we can plan appropriate instruction for a period of critical cognitive growth.

Authentic Instruction

*B*eyond Hands-On assists teachers of young children in planning instruction that is *authentic*, a term used to describe a particular kind of teaching. Authentic instruction can be described in the following ways:

✔ Children are active participants.

✔ Written and oral communication is woven into all disciplines.

✔ Integrated units of instruction take the place of fragmented lesson plans.

✔ Children explore content and ideas for an extended period of time and in a spirit of inquiry.

✔ Assessment is planned to match the type of instruction, and offers a thorough, "growth over time" view of a child's performance.

*T*hus, in a classroom that goes "beyond hands-on," one might expect to see the following teaching practices:

✔ Numerous displays of children's work

✔ Separate area for active, reflective and participative play and work

✔ Publishing center

✔ Blocks and manipulatives

✔ Well-stocked art area

✔ Musical instruments, both commercial and homemade

✔ Cooking center

Ideal "Beyond Hands-On" Classroom

(See Chapter 2 for the rationale for Color Suggestions.)

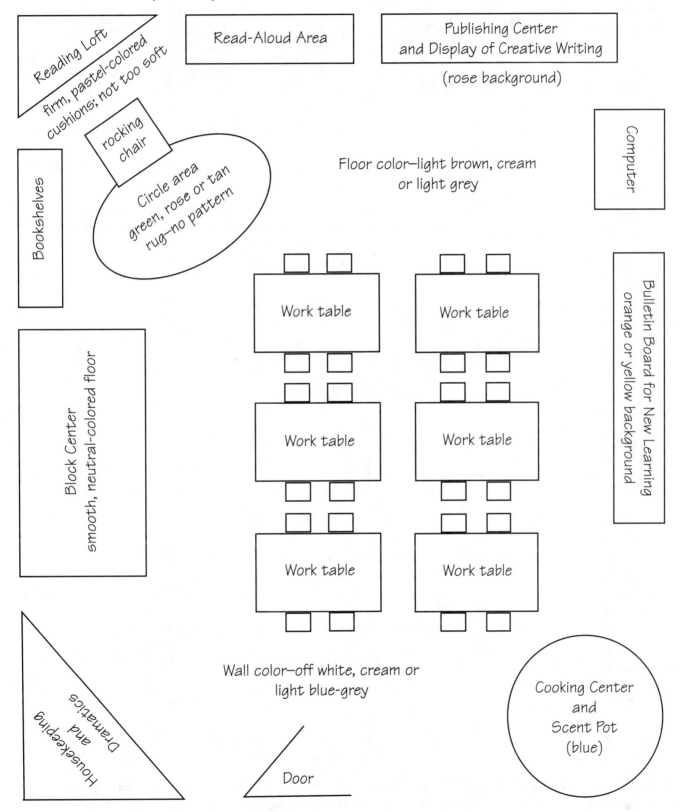

Reading Loft
firm, pastel-colored cushions; not too soft

Read-Aloud Area

Publishing Center
and Display of Creative Writing

(rose background)

rocking chair

Bookshelves

Circle area
green, rose or tan
rug—no pattern

Computer

Floor color—light brown, cream
or light grey

Block Center
smooth, neutral-colored floor

Work table

Work table

Work table

Work table

Work table

Work table

Bulletin Board for New Learning
orange or yellow background

Housekeeping
and
Dramatics

Wall color—off white, cream or
light blue-grey

Door

Cooking Center
and
Scent Pot
(blue)

Name _____

Matrix for Planning "Beyond Hands-On" Instruction

Theme _____ Grade Level _____

	Color	Scent	Taste	Touch	Music
Oral Language					
Written Language					
Logic/Number Tasks					
Gross/Fine Motor Tasks					
Social Development					

Blank copies of this theme planning matrix are provided for your use, beginning on page 135. You can use these pages to design original units and lessons, incorporating the ideas from this book. Be sure to read page 23 and review this sample planning matrix. Additional guidelines for using the blank matrices are on page 134.

How to Use the "Beyond Hands-On" Matrix

Integrated instruction is the key to authentic teaching practices, whether they are hands-on or moving into minds-on techniques. Use the planning matrix to create units that provide for sensory-rich learning experiences. A sample of the matrix, using ideas that will be presented in the book, has been included. Remember that every square of the matrix need not be filled in. This is simply a planning tool, to help you organize your activities with the new information found in *Beyond Hands-On* in mind.

✔ Choose a theme that fits the curriculum guidelines of your school.

✔ Choose a theme that lends itself to hands-on learning.

✔ Plan for one week at a time, but match these weekly units to your long-range plans for the students.

✔ Include assessment-related tasks in the matrix.

✔ Add parent-related tasks to the matrix.

✔ Use action verbs to describe tasks that the students will accomplish. For example: "Students use red markers to write new consonant blends on chart paper," indicates student-generated learning.

Sample of Completed Matrix

Theme _The Alphabet_ **Grade Level** _5-Year-Old Kindergartener_

	Color	Scent	Taste	Touch	Music
Oral Language	Wear restful shades of blue, green or rose when you introduce new words or letters.		Chew peppermints or wintergreen mints as children listen to an alphabet book.		Differentiate between letter sounds by signaling with instruments (page 125).
Written Language	Use orange/yellow marker to write dictated stories or letters.	Use scented markers in citrus or mint to shape letters.		Change the texture of writing tools: chalk, pencils, crayons, markers, pens.	
Logic/Number Tasks		Light a scented candle or spray with pine or wintergreen scent to get children's attention.	Count and sort alphabet-shaped cereals then snack		
Gross/Fine Motor Tasks		Use menthol- or lime-scented shaving cream.		Practice writing letters in chilled shaving cream	Use homemade shakers (page 126) to accompany singing of alphabet songs or chants.
Social Development	Use a neutral or green carpet in a work area as children do alphabet puzzles.			Place soft, earth-colored or rose colored pillows in a reading area—not bright beanbags.	

Tips for Using *Beyond Hands-On*

This book has been organized in four sections: related to the uses of color, scent, taste, touch and sound in the classroom. A brief section containing innovative suggestions for use of music and sound in the classroom completes the book. However, the auditory modality does not receive a great deal of attention in this book, nor is it included in the matrix, because *we typically overuse this modality!* The purpose of *Beyond Hands-On* is to explore the use of the other senses!

	Sight	Touch	Hear	Taste	Smell
Monday	✔				
Tuesday			✔		
Wednesday		✔			
Thursday					✔
Friday				✔	

As you plan curriculum and instruction, consider the following methods:

- ✔ Use the matrix to plan complete units.
- ✔ Try to include a sensory-rich experience each day.
- ✔ Consider one new sensory experience each week.
- ✔ Use specific techniques to meet learning needs of handicapped students.
- ✔ Supplement the curriculum for gifted learners with these ideas.
- ✔ Team up with teachers, and select a "sense" that you each want to become an "expert" on and share your techniques.
- ✔ Implement a school-wide program of *Beyond Hands-On* curriculum.
- ✔ Share your experiences with sensory-rich teaching at a teacher inservice or conference.
- ✔ Invite parents to come into the classroom and assist with these innovations.
- ✔ Simply renew your sense of fun and curiosity in the classroom as you try these techniques.

Chapter 2

The Power of Color in the Classroom

Color, more than any of the other senses, draws on both symbolic and cognitive powers to affect learning. Writing in a provocative piece entitled "Hue and Eye," art historian Louisa Buck probes the intimate relationship between the artist's signature color (such as Van Gogh's "yellow") and his or her message and meaning. For Van Gogh, yellow became an obsession, and he often wrote about seeking the "high yellow note," a quest to paint life in scenes of both health and disease. For Van Gogh, and for the youngsters in your classroom, color conveys more than just . . . color.

The poet Julian Grenfell said, "And *life* is color and warmth and light." He chose the metaphor of color to describe all of life itself; it was that profound. And rightly so. For humans, colors impart

important information, ideals and meanings, so much so that the Chinese say: "Color is emptiness; emptiness is color" (From the Heart Sutra as found in *Living Color*, 1994). Color is everywhere, and imagining life without color is difficult and depressing. Color is part of our vision, our language, our art and our folklore. It is part of what we learn and how we learn it. Yet, as teachers, we know pitifully little about the use of color. Should we know more? Yes.

One might expect artists and poets to concern themselves with color, but what about teachers? We have even more evidence to suggest an investigation of the use of color in our classrooms—especially when young, impressionable children are involved. There's an important reason why.

The research of biopsychologist Sherry Dingman, "suggests that children today are developing awesome capabilities in their right cerebral hemispheres 'at the expense' of the left-hemisphere skills." Apparently, children have been immersed in visual imagery, such as television and video and are therefore quite adept at using the neural systems that carry this kind of information. On the other hand, they have become weak in skills that demand left-hemisphere strengths, such as the ability to "translate a narrative from a book into a visual image in the mind." The home environment has changed substantially. Video (right brain) is king, while books and stories (left-brain language) have been neglected. The result, for classroom teachers, may be children who have difficulty in taking the time or harnessing the skills involved in many language-heavy, left-brain draining activities. We seize the power of the visual and need to use color to stimulate learning. By using color carefully, we may be able to use visual imagery to coax more left-brained language activity. Admittedly, it is an inexact science, more of an art, but definitely worth a try!

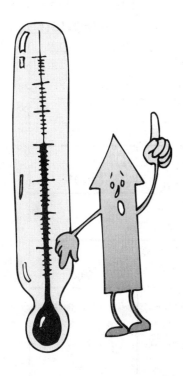

Consider the research that is emerging in the field of color therapy, the use of specific colors to alter moods, attitudes and behavior. Here are a few choice "finds" from the rapidly growing field of color therapy.

✔ Color coding: using a repetition of colors may enhance memory in nursing home residents.

✔ Color may be used to give "cues" to the brain, about where to find information or an object in the classroom.

✔ The deliberate use of color in publications or text can enhance the readability of the narrative. This is especially helpful in breaking text into smaller, more manageable pieces.

✔ Color overlay: 80% of dyslexic children had increased reading comprehension when a blue or grey overlay was placed on the page.

✔ Shades of blue can actually slow down one's heart rate; hence "cardiac blue" is often used in hospitals.

✔ Shades of red can actually increase one's heart rate, and too much red can be down right distracting.

✔ Even intelligence can be colorized: PET scans of "highly intelligent" brains, as measured by tests of abstract reasoning, showed less color as they worked, whereas lower functioning brains showed a great deal of color. Color in PET scans "measures the rate at which the brain uses glucose, its primary fuel." Smarter brains don't have to work as hard; they stay cooler and use less fuel.

Is your brain heating up? Could color become a more important part of your "beyond hands-on classroom"? Could you use color in the environment, in the printed materials or in relationship with other sensory stimuli? Turn to the Color and Cognition Chart on the following page, to review a synopsis of the research on color therapy, and you may find yourself "over the rainbow" with color in your classroom.

Color and Cognition Chart

Color	Excitement	Alertness	Creativity	Reflection	Relaxation	
Black		X				
Blue	X Royal		X Sky	X Aqua	X Pale	
Brown					X Light	
Cream				X	X	
Green			X Jade		X Pale	*Avoid yellow-green*
Grey					X	
Gold	X		X			
Lavender				X	X	
Orange	X	X	X			
Peach				X	X	
Pink				X Warm	X Light	
Purple	X	X	X			
Red	X	X	X			
Rose			X	X	X	
White					X	*Avoid stark whites*

Keep in mind the fact that each person will have a different response to color, influenced by his or her *experiences*. While red might excite *many children*, it could actually *relax* the child who associates the color with his or her favorite stuffed animal or "night night" blanket. Color is an accent for instruction.

28

What the Experts Say About Children and Color

As the footnote to the Color and Cognition Chart states, it is important to think of color as an "accent" to your other instructional methods, much as we use it to decorate a room. With interior design, no amount of color will completely hide the line and form of a cheap sofa or a chipped coffee table! The same goes for teaching. The content and delivery must be in good form, with no chips or breaks; yet color can enhance the instruction, too!

A great deal of research has been done on the psychosocial effects of color on humans. Swiss and German researchers, Luscher, Ostwald, Pfister, Rorschach and Vollmer, conducted detailed studies of the relationships between color and human response. In addition, Rose H. Alschuler and La Berta Weiss Hattwick compiled what is still considered the most important text on the color reactions of children: *Painting and Personality* (1947). And, much of this research is consistent with an entire branch of human psychology: The Gestaltists.

Can an ink blot predict human response? Does a child's choice of crayon color send an implicit message about his or her character? Can a simple color test reveal information about intelligence or personality? Many of the experts mentioned above spent their careers pursuing those questions.

For us, they left a legacy of information and ideas that might make our work as educators more interesting and influential. Here are a few results of studies on color and human response. They may help you in designing your classroom or instruction. Read on for some fascinating facts about color therapy.

Did You Know That . . .

✔ The use of black and white as a color scheme may lower IQ or make children more "dull"?

✔ The careful use of bold colors such as red or orange may increase IQ by as much as 12 points?

✔ In general, cool hues such as blue, are relaxing. Blue windows and walls were often used to help soothe mental patients who are delirious?

✔ Green is often associated with fertility, including "fertile thinking," as in creativity?

✔ Children start out liking yellow as infants but seem to grow less and less fond of it as they mature?

✔ The international "ranking of color preference" is blue, red, green, violet, orange, yellow?

✔ Though the international color ranking holds true (almost) across cultures, a few ethnic groups placed red or orange closer to the front, probably in response to ancient customs or practices involving color?

✔ Color and light have medical, therapeutic implications, hence the use of phototherapy units of blue lights to treat newborns with jaundice, or the use of white light to treat patients with depression because of "winter blues"?

✔ According to Alschuler and Hattwick, "Small children have a natural preference for 'luminous colors such as red, orange, yellow and pink.'"

✔ Brown, black and grey are seldom chosen by children, except to outline? Excessive use of these colors has become an indicator of fear or defiance in their emotional lives.

✱The major source for these quotes is the text: *Color and Human Response,* by Faber Birren, which is noted in the reference section on page 143.

Tips for Color in the Classroom

Use the Color and Cognition Chart on page 28 as a reference guide, but for starters, try to use color to create a classroom environment that is both aesthetically pleasing *and* useful for achieving the kinds of teaching and learning that you want.

Floor Coverings

Neutral or pale tones are best, with the exception of bold or printed rug or tile in the art area. Be careful about boldly colored rugs in the reading circle. They may look cute but could be less effective than a shade of green or blue, which might encourage the children to sit quietly and read or listen to the story.

Bulletin Boards

See pages 45 to 50 and be careful to match the use of the bulletin board with corresponding background and accent colors.

Furniture

Chairs, cushions and seating in the reading area should be in fabrics that use color for reflection or relaxation: peach, rose, aqua blue, light brown, not neon or bold colors.

Walls

Warm, restful colors, in pale tones are best: light green, aqua, peach, cream. Avoid stark white. Avoid bold or dark colors.

Dear Parents, . . .

You can also use color to . . .

✔ Send notes to parents about student progress or behavior (friendly rose or peach)

✔ Send reminders (orange or yellow)

✔ Send requests for donations or assistance in the classroom (friendly green or blue)

✔ Mark areas where care is needed such as the sink, hot plate or science area (orange)

Learn the New Word . . . with Color

Rationale: Bold colors, such as orange, red and shades of lemony yellow demand attention. Reproduce the "learn the word" cards on colored paper, and use black marker to print the words (or letters). Or use white or cream-colored paper, but select markers in a bold shade, to attract the learner's attention. Remember, black and white alone are monotonous.

Just a Stroke of Red (or Orange) for Good Measure

Rationale: Research shows that an occasional bold stroke of red or orange attracts the learner's attention to details. Use this reproducible to create lessons that ask the learner to *mark in red* to identify critical information.

Directions: Color the apple red. Red helps you to remember.

Now use your red crayon or pencil to circle every _____.

_____

_____

_____

_____

_____

_____

_____

_____

_____

_____

The teacher can use the space above to put text, numbers or symbols for the student to mark. For example, you might print a list of words, ask children to mark the blends (bl, sl, sk) or a list of numbers and ask children to mark out groups of five (5).

Name _____

Mark in Red

Use this large apple reproducible to create your own "Mark in Red" lesson.

Name _____

Use this large orange reproducible to create your own "Mark in Orange" lesson.

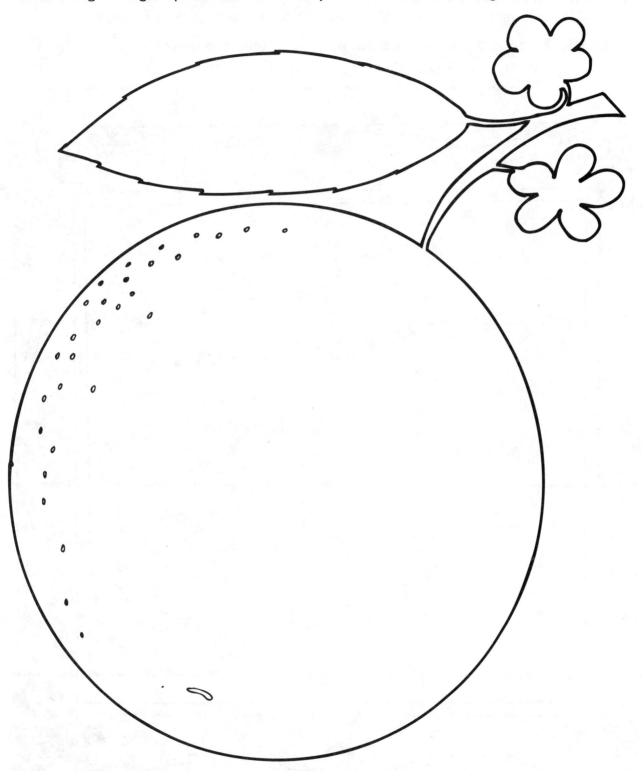

Note: Both red and orange are useful for alerting children to specific points of knowledge or new concepts. How can you *also* incorporate scent or taste in these lessons? See Chapters 3 and 4 for ideas. Use the matrix to plan ahead (page 22).

Color Your World

Rationale: Colors help children to express themselves. Use this reproducible page, along with musical selections from Chapter 5, to create original artwork.

Directions: Listen as the music plays; use your art materials to draw a picture of

_____ .

Original artwork by _____

Name _____

Color for Vocabulary Enrichment

Rationale: Color and color words have symbolic and literary value. Use this knowledge to build fluency in oral language. You may do this activity aloud or as a written activity for older children. How about creating a class *Big Book of Color Words*? You could have two pages for each color, or more if you want, and then compile them into a booklet, using the cover on page 44.

As green as _____

As orange as _____

As orange as _____

As brown as _____

As brown as _____

As purple as _____

As purple as _____

As yellow as _____

As yellow as _____

As red as _____

As red as _____

As blue as _____

As blue as _____

As Colorful as It Can Be

After children complete the pages for "As Colorful as It Can Be," create original booklets by using this page as a cover. You might display this and other work on one of the bulletin boards suggested in the following section.

As Colorful as It Can Be

44

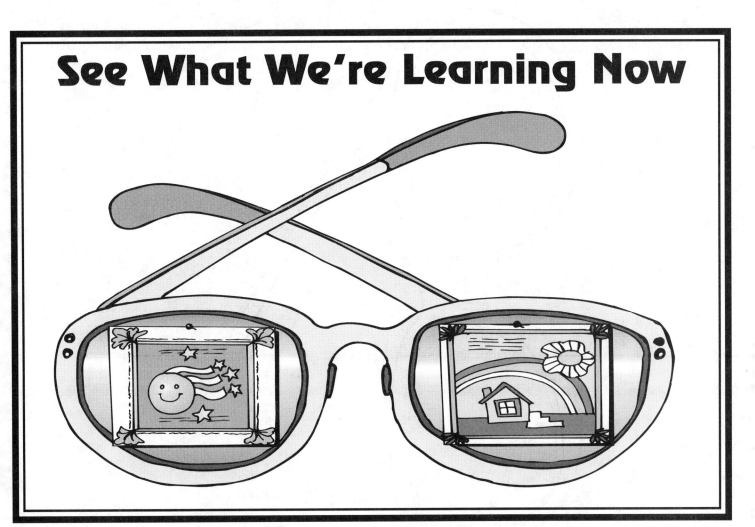

Background Color: yellow or orange

Accent Colors: blue, green, navy

Themes: See What We're Learning Now

Description: Large pairs of spectacles cut out of accent colors with examples of student work placed *inside of them*.

Uses: Make this an interactive board. Children put new work up daily and place the other work in their portfolios.

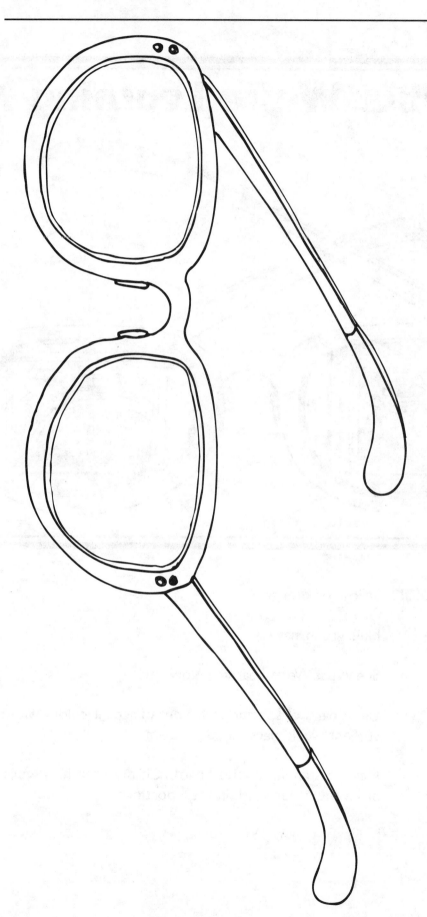

Background Color: jade green, sky blue, warm yellow

Accent Colors: rose and peach

Theme: Growing More Creative Every Day

Description: Intense colored backrground for flowers and flowerpots that have examples of student work.

Uses: creative writing, original artwork, stories, songs, puppets

Try: Use wallpaper samples in bold prints for the flowers, or teach the children to fold tissue paper flowers for a 3-D look.

Bulletin Board Patterns

Light Up the Left Brain with Math

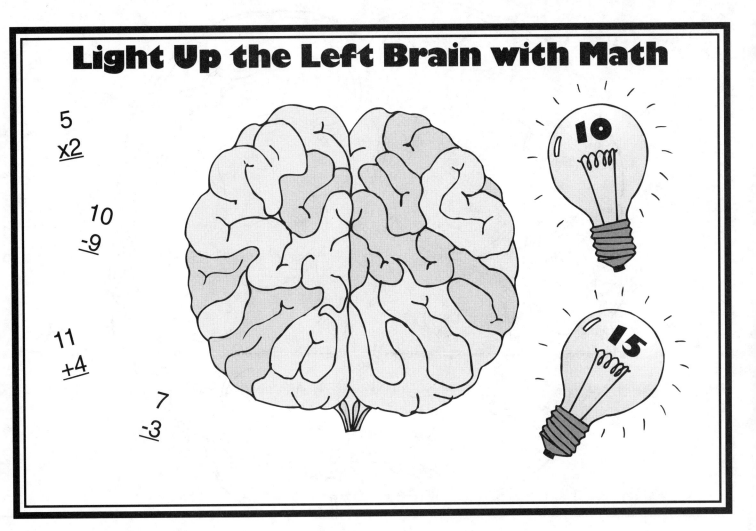

5
x2
___

10
-9
___

11
+4
___

7
-3
___

10

15

Background Color: light green

Accent Colors: warm brown, yellow, aqua

Theme: Light Up the Left Brain with Math

Description: The left side of the brain is used to process math problems. Make this a practice board for math skills. Each problem is written on the "left side" of the brain. Solutions are written on the light bulbs that are stored in a pocket on the board. Children use wipe-off markers to write a solution on a bulb and then Velcro™ or pin it to the "right side" of the brain.

Uses: For drill and practice of skills in any area of mathematics

Bulletin Board Patterns

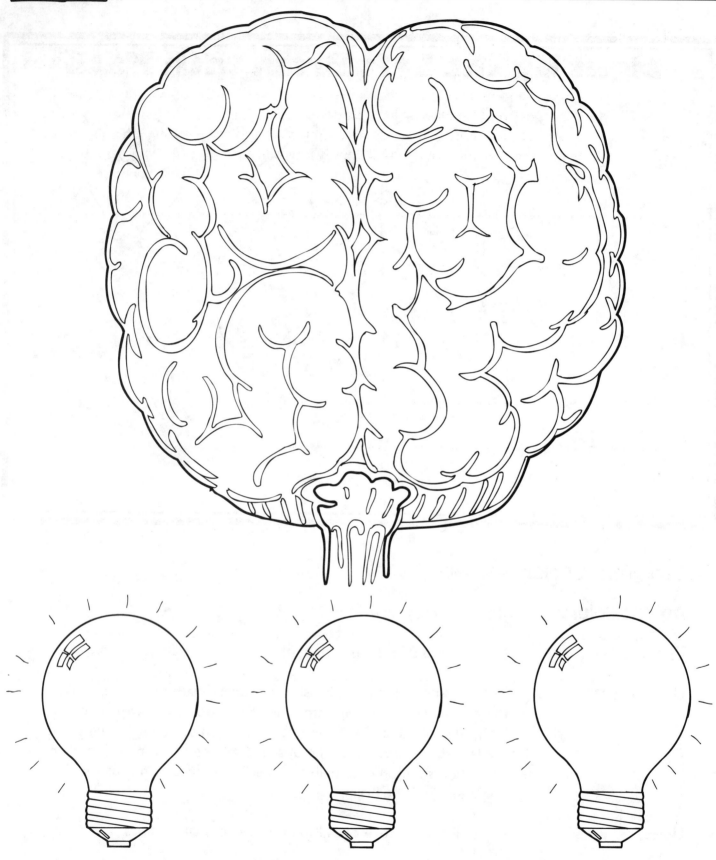

Rationale: Some evidence suggests that children who reverse numbers or letters may have a visual tracking problem that produces dyslexia. Of course, any child who displays serious learning problems should be referred for evaluation, both physical and psychological. For a classroom bandage, reproduce these "blue bandages" on firm blue or light grey paper. You might also fasten the strips to a craft stick to create an easily held tool. Children place the blue bandages under the text or problem that they are working on to help them focus.

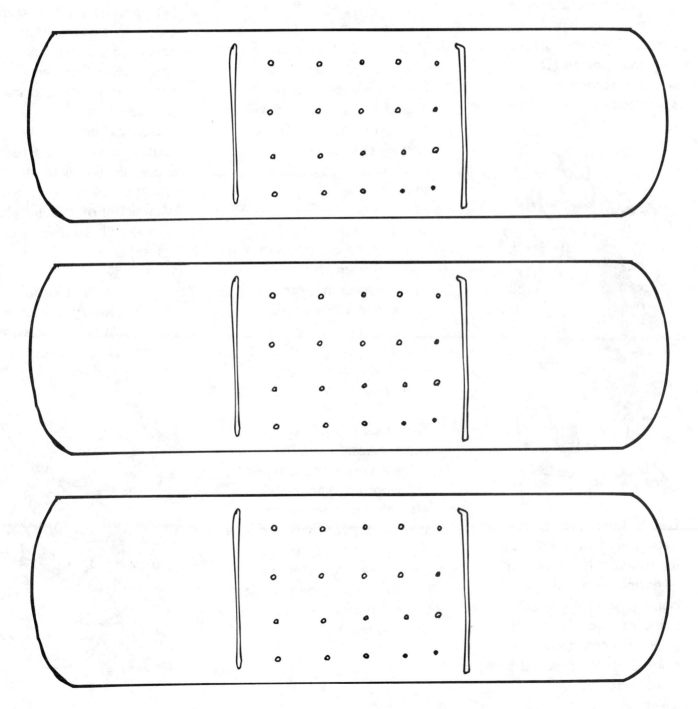

The Personal Touch

Color is an effective mood elixir for adults as well. Typically, we choose colors in clothing, cosmetics and jewelry, that enhance our own complexions, features and ethnic backgrounds. With personal color, the key is to look and feel good. In a profession as demanding as teaching, it is important to alleviate stress in any way that we can. The personal use of color can be a stress-buster.

✔ Get "color-coded" at your department store cosmetics counter. It is free and gives you a professional opinion of what colors make you look (and feel) good. Or check out the book *Color Me Beautiful*, by Carole Jackson.

✔ Wear a bold, bright shade of one of your personal colors on a day that you expect to be tough. It will boost your energy. Think "jewel" colors: jade, ruby, sapphire, even a golden topaz!

✔ Select bold patterns, if only in a scarf or jacket, on days that you want to encourage creativity in an art, drama or writing activity.

✔ Avoid too much black and white. It is sterile and "puts people off."

✔ The book *Living Color*, which presents the use of color according to Chinese philosophy and art, suggests that teachers wear shades of green, blue and pink. Remember that greens are associated with creativity and fertility; while blues and pinks are reflective and restful.

✔ Let your clothing colors reflect the changing seasons. This gives an aura of growth and "fitting in" with the patterns of nature. It also makes you feel good. Change is a boost in itself!

✔ Select foods and snacks in colors that boost your energy. Fruits are a natural choice. See Chapters 3 and 4 for specific information as to why this is so, but condsider a yellow banana (potassium); a red apple (fiber); a glass of grapefruit or orange juice (vitamin C) or tart, purple cranberry juice (infection fighter).

✔ Have fun with color in scarves, jewelry, jackets and hats. You'll send a message to children about your vibrancy and energy!

52

Scents are powerful memory chests, pulling forth thoughts of special encounters and important life experiences. For me, the pungent odor of garlic and tomatoes is forever coupled with the pleasant memories of my Italian grandmother's basement kitchen; while the sharp scent of pine recalls the night in 1989 that Hurricane Hugo felled ten thousand pine trees in my coastal Carolina community. Each of us can recall wonderful or bitter scents and yet, try to think of them *without* the place or circumstance in which you place them. Hard, isn't it? But there's a reason for this. Writing in *A Natural History of the Senses*, Dr. Diane Ackerman notes that each day, "we breathe about 23,040 times and move around 438 cubic feet of air." Each time, we flood our olfactory sites with air and, eventually, our brains with memories attached to those scent-laden wafts of air. The sense of smell might be described as our most primal sense. It kicks into gear just hours after birth; and newborns can quickly "sniff out" their mothers. Though the human animal, in most cases, does not possess a highly developed sense of smell when compared with other creatures, it is still a powerful

force. In fact, researchers at the University of California at Irvine have "theorized that babies incapable of remembering smells might be prone to learning disabilities."

The impact of scent on the learning process, like its cousin taste, has been little investigated. Color, as we say in Chapter 2, has received much more attention. Instead, the research on scent has centered more on its ability to alter feelings of stress as in the study of aromatherapy or in

the pursuit of erotic or romantic results, as in the art of perfume making. However, in recent years, aromatherapy has crossed into fields of medicine and business. Recently, studies into using scents on airplane trips to combat jet lag and in chemotherapy to reduce symptoms of nausea promise important new insights into this area.

Thus, the suggestions for classroom use of scent have been adapted from the ongoing research in aromatherapy and the use of scent to create or change behavior. It holds great promise for teachers. For example, at the University of Cincinnati, researchers found that the scent of *peppermint* caused subjects to become more alert while completing a task. However, there was a critical "educational" side to their findings. The peppermint seemed to work only *after attention had failed*. What a great possibility for teachers of inattentive youngsters! Read on for more suggestions of ways to use scent in the classroom. Refer to the "Scent"sational Aromatherapy Chart on page 55 to select the scent that might work best with your children or situation.

Tips to Remember When Using Scent in the Classroom

✔ Be sure to check children's medical histories for allergies.

✔ Be careful about the use of scent pots and scented candles.

✔ Keep essential oils tightly stored, out of the reach of children.

✔ Be judicious about the use of scent. It is meant to be a subtle enhancement to learning, not a distraction.

✔ Make your use of scents in the classroom a natural, simple experience. It is not meant to be a mood-altering tool, but rather, a biochemical "prompt" for the body.

✔ Share your ideas with parents. Be open about this innovative technique, and make sure that they understand that you are not engaging in some sort of new age "mumbo jumbo," but employing critical new scientific research in your teaching.

Ways to Bring Scent into the Classroom

✔ Baskets or jars of potpourri can be placed near learning centers or areas of activity. Match the desired outcome to an appropriate scent from the chart.

✔ Spray air freshener in the air or into the carpet about 15 minutes *before* the children enter the area. Do not spray scents directly onto children.

✔ Keep an electric scent pot going. Oils, potpourri or special scent pellets can be used in these pots.

✔ Sprinkle essential oils into finger paint or tempera paint to encourage creativity.

✔ Use scented stickers as rewards or incentives.

✔ Use scented markers to heighten the children's attention.

"Scent"sational Aromatherapy Chart

Outcomes

Alertness or Attention	Relaxation or Reflection	Creativity
peppermint	chamomile	sage
wintergreen	jasmine	apple
pine	lavender	rosemary
lemon	sandalwood	rose
eucalyptus	marjoram	basil
spearmint	honeysuckle	cinnamon

Lemons for Learning Language

Reproducible: Use the patterns on page 58 for the lemon.

Rationale: The scent of lemon seems to promote alertness, and the color yellow also seems to have the same effect. So, use the lemon pattern on yellow paper *and* add the scent of lemon to create a favorable situation to introduce new letters, sounds or symbols in the classroom.

Techniques:

✔ Print letters on the lemons and have the children trace them with a citrus-scented marker.

✔ Write new vocabulary words on the lemons and have children glue citrus-flavored cereal circles on the words.

Lemons for Learning Language

✔ Write an initial consonant on a lemon and then let the children work in pairs to find pictures in magazines of objects that begin with the sound. These pictures should be glued on another lemon. Staple, glue or string the two lemons together and hang from the ceiling with clear fishing line.

✔ Use the lemon pattern to make individual glossaries. Children should enter their words in the glossary with a citrus-scented marker or work in an area scented with lemon.

Lemon Patterns

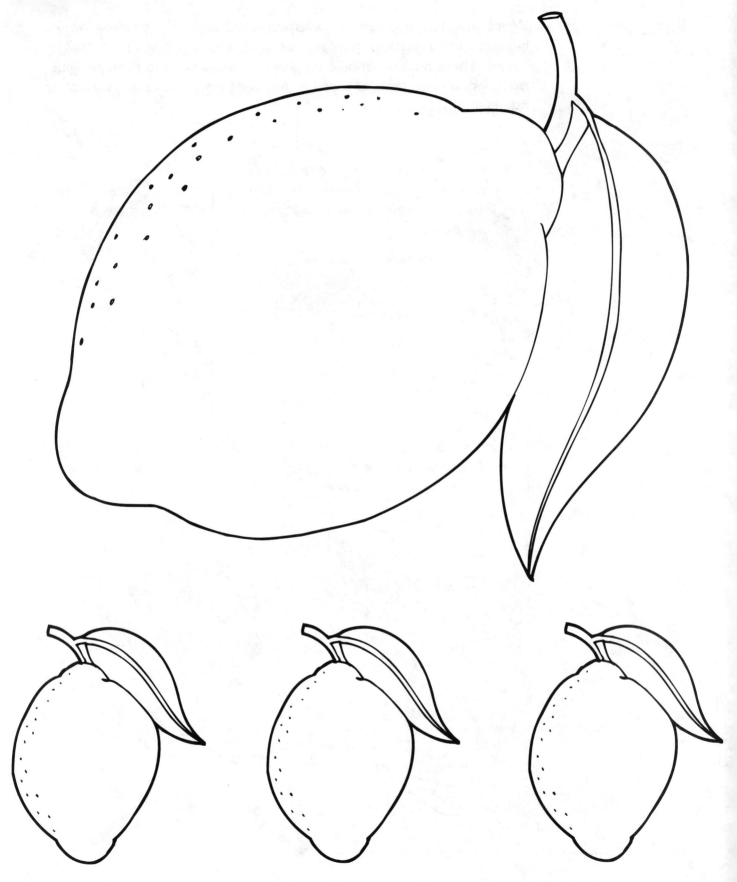

Citrus Cereal

Rationale:

The scent of lemon seems to promote alert and attentive behavior. This is critical when a child is working with numbers. Use the lemon pattern and the scent of lemon on stickers or with lemon-flavored cereal pieces to reinforce the mathematical concepts of counting, sorting, patterning or one-to-one correspondence.

Techniques:

✔ The citrus-fresh scent of fruity cereal rings makes them a good manipulative for sorting and patterning. Use the rings to make patterns or to sort into plastic cups. String them on yarn or use them to create a design on paper.

Lemon-y Learning

✔ Cut out smaller (3" [8 cm]) versions of the lemon pattern or better still, have the children cut them out, for great fine motor practice. Then give each child a plastic bag of 10 "lemons" to use in various counting exercises such as the ones listed below.

1. Write a number or number word on one of the large lemons and pair up children to count out the appropriate number of smaller lemons.

2. Give oral problem-solving tasks that children can solve by using the lemons. For example: If Juan goes to the market to buy 6 lemons but he drops 2 on the way home, how many lemons will be left to make lemonade?

✔ Mix lemon juice in tempera paint and finger-paint the number words or numbers that you are learning. Use one tablespoon (15 ml) lemon juice per cup of paint. You can also do this with language tasks.

✔ Give children small cups of lemonade to sip before you work on math tasks. This is refreshing, and the scent and taste will linger as they attend to their work.

Pinecone Patterns

Note: Use the techniques offered in the lemon section by associating the new letters, words or sound blends with other pungent scents from the "Alertness or Attention" section on the chart on page 55. You can use plain white paper, but be sure to use an attention-grabbing color such as yellow, orange or red marker. If you use a colored paper in a pattern that is designed to match your unit of study, for example, orange pumpkins or green leaves, be sure to use black marker for the best visual appeal.

Note: A reproducible pattern for a pinecone is on page 62 and a pattern for a peppermint is available on page 85 in Chapter 4.

Write your ideas here for using lemon or other attention-grabbing scents to introduce new language skills or to reinforce previously learned skills.

_____

_____

_____

_____

_____

_____

_____

_____

✔ Be sure to include these ideas on your unit planning matrix. See pages 22 and 23 for more about the matrix.

Soothing Scents

Rationale: Sometimes the primary classroom needs to be a quiet, reflective place. This is important during rest time, during silent reading periods and perhaps when the teacher is reading a story aloud for pleasure. You may find that appropriate scents help children relax and reflect and ultimately learn more during the experience. Here are some ideas.

Techniques:

✔ Place an open basket of light floral potpourri near your rocking chair in the circle area. (See page 21 for the ideal classroom.) Keep it covered with a cloth until it is time for reading aloud.

✔ Spray the rest time area with a lavender air freshener before the children lie down. Be careful not to spray their mats or blankets directly.

Hint: Play a tape of ocean sounds for an excellent background to rest time.

Soothing Scents

✔ Keep a bar of honeysuckle or sandalwood soap in the classroom and encourage children to wash their hands with it before they spend time in the reading center. The scent on their hands will encourage relaxation and quiet behavior as they handle the books or magazines.

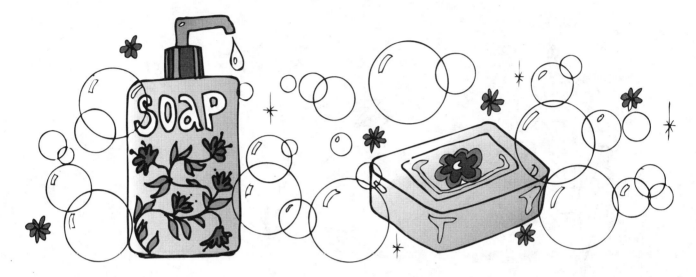

✔ Give children cups of warm chamomile tea, sweetened with honey, as a treat before they rest or reading time. This is a good idea after a particularly busy or active morning. This tasty tea goes well with a handful of animal crackers.

Hint: Remember that chamomile tea was the drink of choice in *The Tale of Peter Rabbit*, used to lull naughty rabbits to sleep!

Soothing Scents

Techniques: ✔ Children can trace and cut the honeysuckle and lavender patterns and then color them. Decorate the reading center or other quiet areas with homemade vines or restful flowers, sprayed with scent.

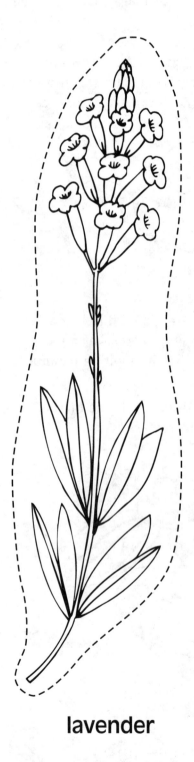

lavender

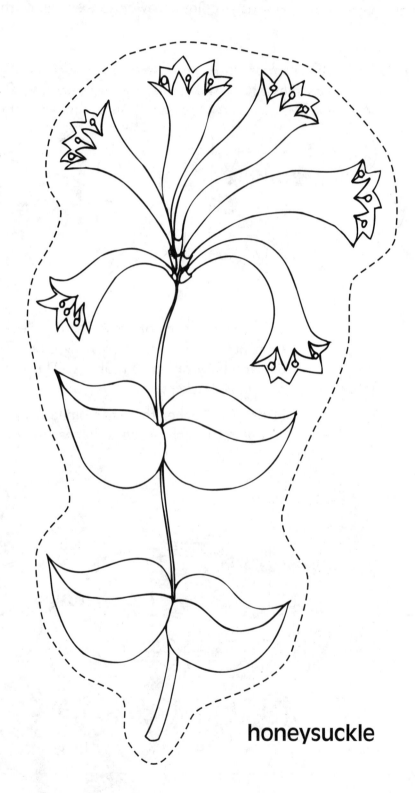

honeysuckle

"Scent"sational Learning for Creative Times

Creativity . . . the spice that makes learning such a pleasure and *spices* do seem to enhance creative feelings. Look at the chart on page 55 to see how cinnamon and sage can ignite creative sparks. Though it is not listed, ginger is also a nice scent for creative classrooms. Thus the pattern for a gingerbread man is on page 69.

Rationale: The scent of ginger and cinnamon, though slightly acrid, send a powerful sensory message to the limbic system. They have a similar impact on taste, and so the two senses mix beautifully in a number of the techniques suggested here.

✔ Sprinkle cinnamon or ginger in tempera paint at the easel or in finger paint. Use one teaspoon (5 ml) per cup of paint.

"Scent"sational Learning for Creative Times

✔ Enjoy a snack of gingersnaps or cinnamon-dusted graham crackers before a writing or creative arts lesson. Perhaps ginger ale and cinnamon drops would make a nice treat while children write in their journals, a time for creative minds to open up.

✔ Simmer some basil or sage in the scent pot and place near the art center or work area for publishing. (See the ideal classroom on page 21.)

Gingerbread Creativity

Techniques: Use the patterns for the gingerbread man and apple on page 69 whenever you wish to promote a creative flow of ideas in the classroom. Remember, the scent that you spray on these papers or use in the area, should enhance creativity. And don't limit your own creativity. Consult the Color and Cognition Chart on page 28 to see how these patterns can be colored or reproduced to make full use of a sensory experience.

✔ Use the patterns for a creative writing exercise.

✔ Use the patterns as an easel for drawing or painting.

✔ Use the patterns as postcards to send to pen pals.

✔ Use the patterns to make original books.

✔ Use the patterns as mini story boards for math problems.

Rationale: The scent of rose seems to invoke creativity. Reproduce the rose pattern, which has been provided in both lined and unlined versions (page 72), to serve as the pages for individual *A Garden of Thoughts* journals. Children can write poems, stories or ideas in these journals, or share their experiences. Again, consult the Color and Cognition Chart on page 28 to make the most "sense" of this idea!

Rose Pattern

The Personal Touch

Both men and women use scents to convey personal messages. Many of us enjoy wearing a "signature scent" as well. For adults, wearing cologne, perfume or after shave brings pleasure. That's as it should be. However, we might stop to consider if our perfume distracts children from the tasks at hand. Perhaps we might infuse some teaching power into the choices that we make about perfume and cologne in the classroom! Just for fun, visit your toiletries counter and match up some scents that enhance the kind of teaching that is your goal for a particular day!

If your goal is to:

✔ introduce new learning

✔ reinforce a particularly difficult concept

✔ keep the children's attention during an outdoor activity or field trip

✔ work with a large group, rather than small groups or individual children

Then your fragrance should be:

✔ strong and pungent

✔ deep and woodsy

✔ bright and fruity

Your favorite brand might be

_____

If your goal is to:

✔ offer a quiet and relaxing day

✔ work in small groups on reflective kinds of tasks

✔ spend a lot of time reading aloud

✔ talking and working one on one with writing projects

✔ doing assessment of learning

Then your fragrance should be:

✔ gentle and floral

✔ a subtle spice

✔ soft with sandalwood

Your favorite brand might be

_____

The Personal Touch

If your goal is:

✔ active and creative teaching

✔ an arts-related lesson

✔ transfer of old learning to a fresh situation

Then your fragrance should be:

✔ spicy and provocative

✔ crispy with apple

✔ rich with rose scent

Your favorite brand might be

_____

Scent can be a simple, yet effective way for you, the teacher, to enhance your own mood or creative energy. Think of scent in the classroom in two ways: to serve as a biochemical "prompt" for student learning and as a technique for making your own life richer and more pleasant. For those of you who are prone to tension headaches, for example, a few drops of oil of peppermint rubbed in at the temples can quickly ease the pain.

What primary school teacher doesn't have a recipe for homemade applesauce? Cooking in the classroom offers some of the best hands-on instruction, but what about going "beyond hands-on"? How does the sense of *taste* serve as a learning enhancer? How can taste, in the form of cooking and eating activities, improve the acquisition of knowledge? Creative output? Reflective thinking?

contexts and messages which are difficult to separate. For teachers, that is good news. Our work becomes easier when we can reinforce knowledge and concepts in a variety of modalities. By harnessing the sense of taste to reinforce learning, we place nearly 10,000 taste buds at our disposal, each one carrying about 50 taste cells that alert neurons to carry messages to the brain. And what messages do the taste buds send to the brain?

Clearly, many of the messages are closely linked to the related sense of smell (Chapter 3). So a number of the activities in this chapter will contain a variation of ideas that were shared in Chapter 3. However, this section also draws on some of the more recent studies of how foods may influence one's mood. With young children, moods and accompanying attitudes can be powerful learning enhancers.

According to Dr. Diane Ackerman (*A Natural History of the Senses*), the sense of taste is "largely social," meaning that it is most often, and best served in the company of other people. Tastes, and the foods that convey the flavors, have important social

Taste the Learning

reason that "Taste the Learning" could be helpful in going beyond hands-on in our teaching. It is an opportunity to impress both emotional and cognitive behavior.

Refer to the Taste the Learning Chart on page 77 to see how specific tastes may be helpful in shaping behavior. Remember, too, how simple "behaviorism" (that is, the use of food as a reward) can also be a powerful tool in the classroom. Of course, we shouldn't be passing out chocolate drops like food pellets for rats in the laboratory! However, taste is one of the strongest human reactions. Use it to enhance learning in a classroom that goes beyond hands-on, into minds-on instruction.

Note: Before offering any food to your students, make sure you are aware of any allergies or dietary restrictions your students may have.

Taste and scent may have an impact on the limbic system, that portion of the brain that, according to the *Human Brain Coloring Book* (M.C. Diamond, et al), "is also known as the visceral or emotional brain, concerned with behavioral and emotional expression." It is interesting to note that the limbic system is involved with such primal matters as feeding patterns, flight and fight behavior and repro- duction, but also seems to be involved in *memory processing*! Do you see the connection? Taste, like all other senses, must travel through the limbic system, which receives "samples of all incoming sensory information." Therefore, the sensory information may have an effect on memory, as in memory retention or storage of new information in the memory. This limbic system connection is one

Taste the Learning Chart

Taste or Food Source	Possible Influence on Behavior or Mood
Carbohydrates	Release endorphins: quiet, tranquil mood. Too much at lunch, and the children will nod off. Save these for afternoon snack time.
Protein	Delivers energy jolt to the system. Feeds the brain. Good for morning snack time.
Vanilla	Calm, reflective mood enhancer
Peppermint	Attention-grabber; may help retrieve information from memory
Ginger or Cinnamon	Calms nausea; enhances creativity
Apple	Natural sweet for energy, with a scent that promotes creativity
Orange	Energy jolt with a color and scent that make a complete "alertness" package
Almond	Enormous protein boost with a scent that is relaxing as well. Good snack for precooperative group lesson.

Apple, Almond, Raisin Salad

Rationale:
The taste, scent, texture and color of this treat deliver a "wake up" call to the brain. It is an excellent morning snack, designed to build up the learning curve during the critical morning hours of instruction. However, this activity also provides practice in mathematical concepts of estimating and problem solving. Use the Problem-Solving Work Area sheet on page 79 to assess children's performance in this task.

Ingredients:

sliced red and green apples (skins on)*

1/4 cup (60 ml) of raisins for each child

I cup (240 ml) of silvered almonds

I tsp. (5 ml) cinnamon or ginger

*You will need one apple for every three children.

Task:
Children should wash their hands and the work table area first.

Working in pairs, children mix the ingredients in a large mixing bowl.

Children in first grade or higher can also measure all ingredients from the boxes or bags.

Sprinkle the mixture with cinnamon or ginger and stir well.

Concept:
Hand out paper cups and challenge the children to figure out how to *equally* divide the mixture so that every person can try the snack.

Inquiry Questions:
What should you do first?
Can you think of any tools that might help you?
What do we mean by *equal*?
How can we work together to do this?
Can you think of a different way to figure this out?

78

Name _____

Problem-Solving Work Area

Date: _____

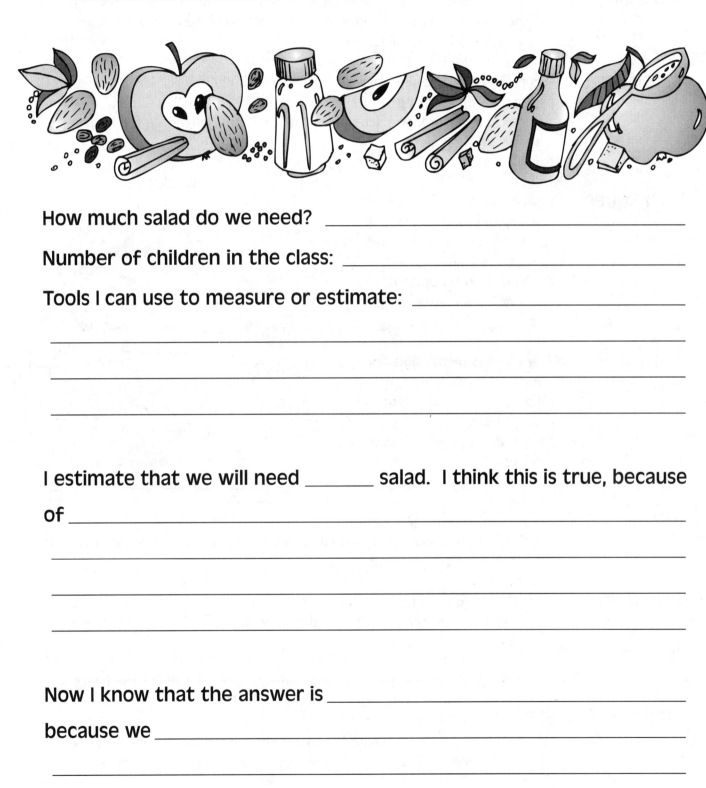

How much salad do we need? _____

Number of children in the class: _____

Tools I can use to measure or estimate: _____

_____

_____

_____

I estimate that we will need _____ salad. I think this is true, because

of _____

_____

_____

_____

Now I know that the answer is _____

because we _____

_____

_____

"Orange" You Glad It Is Science Time?

Rationale: The color, scent and taste of orange make it a natural learning tool. Use this incentive to create an observation on the way that matter changes when temperature is adjusted.

Materials: 1 cup (240 ml) of chilled orange juice for each child
paper cups for drinking
3 cups (720 ml) orange juice plus 2 cups (480 ml) ginger ale for freezing
ice trays with dividers
toothpicks or craft sticks

Techniques: Divide the class into two laboratory teams. Team one is responsible for pouring and serving the chilled juice and for handing out copies of the observation sheet on page 81 and orange crayons.

Team two is responsible for pouring the orange-ginger ale mixture into ice trays and placing it into the freezer. *After 45 minutes of freezing time, toothpicks or craft sticks must be inserted for skewers.

*A timekeeper should be assigned to set and watch the timer or clock for 45 minutes, time to insert skewers.

Instruction: Print the words: *matter, solid, liquid, gas, cold* and *freeze* on the board, or better still, on a chart, using scented orange marker. Discuss these terms prior to the activity time.

Step 1: Children sip the cold juice and complete the questions on the observation sheet.

Step 2: Children observe and then eat the frozen juice cubes and then complete the items on the observation sheet.

80

Name _____

"Orange" You Glad It Is Science Time?

Date: _____

Task 1: Describe the cold orange juice. How did it look and feel? You can draw a picture or write your answer. _____

_____

```



```

Task 2: Was the juice a solid or a liquid? How do you know this?

_____

_____

_____

Task 3: What happended to the juice after it went into the freezer?

_____

_____

_____

Task 4: Describe the juice after it was frozen? You can draw it, too.

_____

_____

Using words from the vocabulary list and pictures that you draw, tell what you know about how things change when they are frozen. Why?

_____

_____

_____

Quiet Time Cereal Snack: A High Carbohydrate Relaxer

Rationale: Use this snack as a prelude to reading a story aloud to the children. The subtle flavors, texture or chewing and nutrients will relax them. See the suggestions for scent and color on pages 31 and 54 for use in read-aloud areas.

Techniques: Children should mix this snack in a large sealable, plastic bag.

Mix two cups (480 ml) each of the following: square-shaped, whole grain cereal, fruit-filled cereal squares, puffed rice cereal, oat ring cereal.

Note: None of the cereals should have added sugar or frosting. Use generic store brands for a wholesome but less expensive cereal.

(Optional) Add 1 cup (240 ml) toasted coconut and peanut pieces. Shake well.

Serve: The snack should be served in white paper cups that the children have decorated with scenes from "what they think the story will be about." Share the title of the book, then pass out markers and crayons. While the "helpers" mix the snack, others can design their cups.

Extension: Extend this activity by using the Reading Reflection Page (page 83) after reading the story aloud.

Name _____

The name of this story is _____.

The author of this story is _____.

An illustrator named _____ drew the art for this story.

This is a good story because _____

_____

_____

Here is a picture about the story.

Two words that describe this story are _____

and _____.

Peppermints for Powerful Learning

Rationale: The scent and taste of peppermint seem to "pep up" the brain, making children more alert. What a great opportunity to introduce new concepts, take a quiz or do an assessment!

Techniques: Offer peppermint lozenges for children to suck on as they learn new letters or sounds. (Not recommended for small children for whom hard candy may pose a chocking hazard.)

or

Give the children peppermint or wintergreen-scented markers to highlight words that they have written on a chart story or in their journals.

or

Use peppermint candies as math manipulatives to be counted and matched as you teach number concepts.

or

Heat oil of peppermint in a scent pot as you give new instruction or do an assessment.

or

Swirl peppermint flavor into milk at snack time to brighten attitudes.

Uses: The reproducible peppermint candy on page 85 can be used for a writing activity, such as practicing spelling or vocabulary words. Children can cut out the 10 small mints for use as math manipulatives.

Cheese, Please Geometry

Rationale: Slices of yellow cheese provide a colorful incentive for the senses. The protein lift is critical to learning.

Techniques: Spread the work area with waxed paper.

Place cookie cutters in circle, square, diamond, triangle, rectangle and oval shapes in a basket or margarine tub.

Children should wash their hands and then use the cookie cutters to practice cutting slices of cheese with the cutters.

Children can match the cheese shapes to crackers that have the same shape.

Materials: cookie cutters in geometric shapes (spray with non-stick vegetable cooking spray first)
two slices of cheese per child (four shapes)
crackers in geometric shapes
waxed paper

Extend this activity with the Cut and Paste Shape Page on page 87.

Rationale: After snacking on the high protein cheese, complete this activity which reinforces the names and designs of shapes. What colors could also help to reinforce this lesson? Refer to Chapter 2.

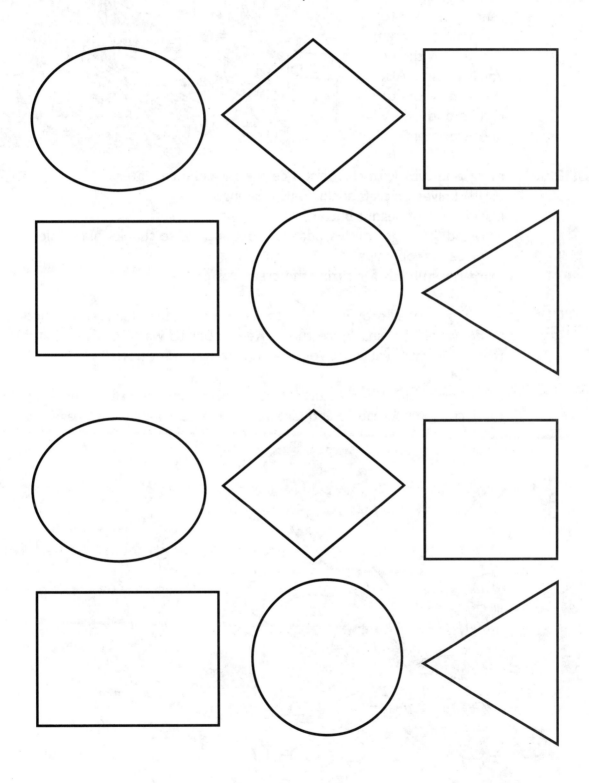

Creative Snacking: Carrot, Celery, Peanut Butter Creatures

Rationale: Fresh vegetables and peanut butter offer an energy lift by sending protein to the brain and vitamins A and C to the nervous system. Also, the bold colors of carrots and celery enhance attention.

Materials: margarine tubs with carrot and celery sticks in ice water
plastic knives or craft sticks for spreading
plastic cups of peanut butter
assorted toppings: raisins, peanuts, coconut, pickle chunks, pineapple pieces, carob chips
margarine tub lids for sitting the creatures on

Techniques: Working in small groups of four to six at a time, the children are encouraged to design original snack creatures. Remember to wash hands first and to teach: You must eat what you use. Waste not; want not!

Note: After completing the creatures, extend this lesson to writing and art by using the Picture My Creature and Creature Verse reproducible on page 89.

Name _____

Picture My Creature

Draw your creature . . .

Write about your creature . . .

Creature Verse

A celery and carrot _____ that is what I made.

It is bigger than a _____.

I am not afraid!

With arms like _____ and a tail of power.

You will eat up my _____ in less than one hour!

Listen and Snack . . . A Fun Way to Follow Directions

Rationale: Vanilla is a relaxing flavor, so vanilla frosting is used in this recipe for learning to follow oral directions.

Ingredients: one tub of vanilla frosting
plastic knives or craft sticks for
    spreading
graham crackers (one large cracker per child)
red cinnamon candies
pretzel sticks (two per child)

Techniques: This is best done in small groups of four to six children at a time. Prepare the work area by spreading waxed paper on the table and setting out ingredients in baskets or on a tray.

Read the directions aloud.

1. Take one graham cracker and place it in front of you.
2. Using a plastic knife or craft stick, cut the cracker in fourths (demonstrate). You will have four rectangles.
3. Spread pieces with vanilla frosting.
4. Place one cracker piece in front of you.
5. Use pretzel sticks to make antlers on your animal.
6. Use cinnamon candies to make the nose, eyes and mouth.
7. What animal did you make? (deer or reindeer)

Anytime Following Directions Snack Story

Rationale: Choose a high protein, colorful snack treat that can be easily picked up and munched or manipulated as part of the story. Learning to follow oral directions is an important primary grade skill. Fill in the blanks to create your own story. Improvise and use this often in the planning matrix.

Choose _____ of the _____ and place

them on your _____. Now _____ with

_____ of the pieces. How many are left? Take those pieces, and

put them in order from _____ to _____.

Now take _____ more pieces and _____ with

them. Do you have enough to _____? Now you may eat

_____ of the pieces. With the rest, try to _____.

Now, take a piece of paper and draw _____. Put

_____ of the pieces of _____ in it. Draw a pic-

ture of yourself next to the _____. Give yourself a

_____ and a _____ and a big, hungry mouth.

You may finish eating the snack. Good listening.

Name _____

Recipe Card to Send Home

From the Classroom of _____

Chef: _____

We made: _____

You will need: _____

_____

_____

_____

_____

_____

You will do: _____

_____

_____

_____

Don't forget to: _____

_____

_____

92

The Personal Touch

Children need lots of high protein, color-rich foods to feed their growing brains. As adults, we need less growth and more nurturing. Taste is often an antithesis of nurturing. We focus on cravings, such as the need for chocolate or caffeine and ignore the power of taste to nurture us as care givers of children. Here are some simple, yet effective "taste the learning" or better still, "taste the nurturing" ideas for adults.

✔ For a quick pep up: ginger or lemon tea with honey

✔ For a headache: peppermint tea

✔ For a sore throat: thyme tea heavily laced with honey

✔ For nausea: ginger ale or ginger capsules, wintergreen lozenges

✔ For quick energy: dried pineapple and nuts

✔ Low-fat snack: popcorn sprinkled with onion and garlic powder

✔ To prevent colds: vitamin C capsules, cranberry juice

✔ Stress-buster: chamomile tea, tea sprinkled with rosemary, celery juice for neuralgia

Tasty Ideas

Can you think of new ways to enhance learning through the sense of taste? Write them here, or place them on the matrix for the unit that you are designing. For more on the matrix, see page 22.

_____

_____

_____

_____

_____

_____

To begin using the "Taste the Learning" techniques, make a list of materials and ingredients that you would like to add to your classroom.

Staples	Spices	Utensils

Letter to Parents or Care Givers

Dear Parents or Care Givers,

As you might have noticed, I am introducing some interesting new techniques for using scent and taste to enhance learning. Children seem to respond to this instruction and that is my goal. However, this kind of teaching requires lots of materials other than pencils, paper and crayons. Perhaps you would like to help by sharing one or more of the items on the Grocery List below. Your help is appreciated. Join us in the classroom and see how taste and scent can make a difference in children's attention, creativity and time for reflection.

Thank you,

_____

Teacher

Grocery List for _____'s Class

Week of _____   Theme: _____

We will need _____

_____

_____

Yes, I can bring _____

_____

Parent's or Care Giver's signature _____

Chapter 5

Touching Creativity

"A BLOCK"

brand names, as well as a renewal of interest in Montessori Pre-Schools, cooking in the classroom and block play bring tactile learning into the spotlight. On the cutting edge, computer technology and the boldly innovative and tactile-rich Reggio Emilia style of instruction offer yet another glimpse of the possibilities of tactile teaching.

Still, we must think of tactile or "high touch" instruction as more than just "that other modality." What possibilities does this modality have for going "beyond hands-on" in teaching? Perhaps the answer is enhancing CREATIVITY!

As a novice teacher, one of the first axioms of good instruction that I learned was: "Cover the three modalities of learning: auditory, visual and tactile." As good little pre-teachers, we dutifully prepared lesson plans that *looked like* they covered all three of the modalities, and then were shocked and dismayed at how foreign the "tactile" modality was to our master teachers in the schools. As interns and first-year teachers, I remember that many of my cohorts resorted to the visual and auditory modalities only (pencil and paper and lecture), abandoning that precious and

valuable teaching tool: the tactile modality. Today, there is a new and growing commitment to multi-modality teaching. Programs such as Math Their Way, AIMS, Fast Science, to name a few

In the 1993 work, *Creating Minds*, Dr. Howard Gardner, who has been studying the emergence of intelligence and creativity for 25 years at Harvard University's Project Zero, decided to explore the phenomena of creative genius, by "looking for patterns" in the lives of seven great artists and scientists. He was looking for the roots of creative output, for the mind that is not satisfied with a pat answer, but seeks for divergent, fresh, unusual answers. What he found is fascinating and pretty intense, but it is safe to say for our purposes as teachers of young children, that what we do in the early years of learning is critical and influential. Gardner says:

The quality of these early years is crucial. If, in early life, children have the opportunity to discover much about their world and to do so in a comfortable, exploring way, they will accumulate invaluable "capital of creativity" on which they can draw later in life. If, on the other hand, children are restrained from such discovering activities, pushed in only one direction, or burdened with the view that there is only one correct answer or that correct answers must be meted out only by those in authority, then the chances that they will ever cast out on their own are significantly reduced. (p. 31)

What a challenge for the "beyond hands-on" classroom! It is not enough to simply provide lots of paint, beads, colored pasta and math manipulatives. We must *design an environment* that deliberately and carefully encourages creativity. That is not easy when so many time constraints and testing parameters constantly nip at our heels. However the knowledge that children need time, materials and encouragement to build up a "capital of creativity" can help us to carve out our own niche in teaching.

Materials List for High-Touch Teaching

- ❏ balls
- ❏ baskets (for sorting)
- ❏ beads
- ❏ beans (dried, all kinds)
- ❏ bells
- ❏ bins
- ❏ blocks
- ❏ bottle caps
- ❏ bubbles
- ❏ buttons
- ❏ clay
- ❏ cookie cutters
- ❏ crackers
- ❏ craft sticks
- ❏ crayons
- ❏ dish detergent (for bubbles)
- ❏ empty boxes (all sizes)
- ❏ fabric (all kinds)
- ❏ felt
- ❏ flour
- ❏ food coloring
- ❏ gelatin
- ❏ glitter
- ❏ glue
- ❏ glue gun
- ❏ hole punch
- ❏ jars
- ❏ jewels (costume, junk)
- ❏ junk (for sorting)
- ❏ paint (finger, tempera)

- ❏ paper (colored and plain)
- ❏ parquetry blocks
- ❏ pasta (all kinds, dried)
- ❏ paste
- ❏ plastic animals and dinosaurs
- ❏ Polaroid™ type camera
- ❏ popcorn
- ❏ pudding mix
- ❏ puppets
- ❏ puzzles
- ❏ rice
- ❏ safety scissors
- ❏ salt
- ❏ sand
- ❏ scented markers
- ❏ shaving cream
- ❏ sponges
- ❏ stickers
- ❏ string
- ❏ tools
- ❏ typewriter
- ❏ used greeting cards
- ❏ vegetables (raw for prints)
- ❏ waffle blocks
- ❏ wallpaper samples
- ❏ water
- ❏ wood
- ❏ yarn
- ❏ zip-type plastic bags

Clean-Shave for Smooth Thinking

Rationale: Shaving cream offers an inexpensive yet stimulating medium for enhancing learning and creativity. Choose the menthol or mint scents to further entice the senses and cognition.

Description: Spray a thick layer of chilled shaving cream on waxed paper or on an old shower curtain (floor), on a picnic tabletop (outdoors) that has been covered with newspaper. Use it to:

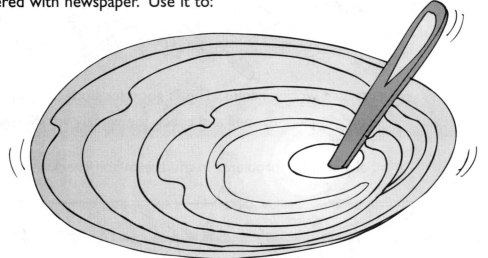

✔ Illustrate the blending of colors or to practice making color families by mixing food coloring drops into the cream.

✔ Imprint objects, such as shells, leaves, rocks to make "instant fossils" and to help learn the names of new objects by making a tactile connection.

✔ Draw "pictures" in the snow to go along with a unit on winter or seasons.

✔ Practice writing names. This is good for both print or cursive letters.

✔ Work in pairs to spell and check the weekly vocabulary words or spelling list.

✔ Solve number problems in the cream and check them with a calculator.

✔ Use cookie cutters to imprint geometric shapes and then learn the names.

Your idea: _____

_____

Your idea: _____

_____

Your idea: _____

_____

Rebus Stories with a New Twist

Rationale: The rebus story has long been an effective teaching tool. One simply inserts a picture to represent a word. But with so many kinds of stickers on the market, especially fuzzy, furry, glitter, neon or scented stickers, the opportunity for high-touch learning becomes huge!

Description: Use the reproducible on page 102 to create original rebus stories. Be sure to provide a wide variety of stickers that go along with the theme or unit. See matrix on page 22.

Hints:

✔ Keep the stickers in folders or sealed margarine tubs, organized by themes: animal stickers, nature stickers, people stickers, planet stickers.

✔ Use recycled file folders, cut into one-half pieces, to "mount" your pages.

✔ See Chapters 2 and 3 for ideas for using color and scent as the children create rebus stories or books.

✔ Place the rebus books on one of the display boards described on pages 45 to 50.

✔ Put the rebus books into a creative arts portfolio cover. See page 104.

✔ Give the children adequate *time* to create something like this. It cannot be rushed.

✔ Always review vocabulary words before beginning such an activity.

✔ Encourage children to share their rebus stories, either with a partner, parent volunteer or with a teacher. Creativity needs open, lavish, *encouragement!*

Rebus Story Patterns

Collect Creative Efforts in Portfolios

Portfolio assessment can be non-graded. Experts in creativity suggest that creativity flourishes when there are few "expectations" or rules.

Portfolio assessment is a national trend.

Portfolio assessment teaches children to be responsible for their own work and to take pride in what will be saved.

Portfolios are a natural, "artistic" outgrowth of creative work.

Make a creativity portfolio out of . . .

✓ clean pizza boxes (use portfolio cover on top)

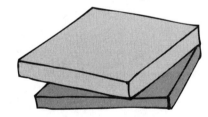

✓ recycled accordion files from a business

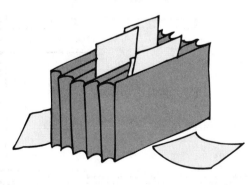

✓ used typing paper boxes

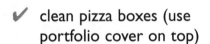

✓ sturdy brown paper shopping bags that children decorate

✓ inexpensive plastic baskets that can be stacked and which can hold 3-D efforts, such as clay, collage or larger items

Catch Me Being
CREATIVE

_____
Name

Catch Me Being Creative Response Page

I like this work because _____

_____

_____

_____

This is different than other work because _____

_____

_____

_____

Three words that tell about this work are:

_____, _____, _____

I am a creative person because _____

_____

_____

_____

Teacher's Comments: This work shows creativity in _____

_____

_____

_____

Beef Up the Block Center

Rationale: Blocks may be one of the most *classic, valuable and underused* materials in the primary school. Dollar for dollar, a good set of plain classroom blocks lasts longer than almost any other item. Moreover blocks offer a rich, diverse, beyond hands-on medium for enhancing learning.

Description: You can use blocks to reinforce new skills, such as counting or making number patterns, or to generate verbal fluency, by describing the size, shape or design of a block creation. Block play is a perfect method for increasing activity between *left and right brain!*

Why don't you . . .

✔ Expand your block center to include some of the items listed on the next page?

✔ Extend the amount of time or opportunity for block play several times each week?

✔ Experiment with "girls only" and "boys only" block time to encourage girls to increase the time that they spend in this center? Research indicates that girls may avoid the block center because of the rough play that is so much a part of little boys' learning.

✔ Enter selected manipulatives, such as plastic animals or dinosaurs into the block center, to go along with your unit theme.

✔ Earn extra "block time" as a reward in your classroom? This will demonstrate how much you value it.

✔ Expect that block play can be messy, and just relax and enjoy it?

✔ Enjoy children's creative efforts in the block center, and remember that creativity is often nurtured by an adult who accepts and encourages divergent responses?

✔ Establish a block center in your second or third grade classroom? Bold move!

Item	Dare I Try It?		Source
Empty salt boxes	Yes	No	
Empty wrapping paper rolls	Yes	No	
Clean paper milk cartons of various sizes	Yes	No	
Cookie tins of many shapes and colors (nice and noisy)	Yes	No	
Spools of many sizes	Yes	No	
Margarine and whipped topping tubs (lids on)	Yes	No	
Recycled stationery boxes with tops	Yes	No	
Clean pizza delivery boxes (sealed)	Yes	No	
shoe boxes	Yes	No	
Cereal boxes	Yes	No	
Laundry soap boxes	Yes	No	
Diaper wipes containers (lids on)	Yes	No	

Block Center Checklist for Assessment

Student	Skills	Rating

Rating Key: **CC:** *Clearly Creative:* Bold, divergent thinking, long attention span. Transfers new learning to the block center easily.

MC: *Moderately Creative:* Occasionally tries new ideas, good attention span, practices new learning with guidance.

LC: *Less Creative:* May be afraid to try new ideas, often mimics other children, needs direction and encouragement often. Easily frustrated, brief attention span.

Mosaics

Rationale: The mosaic is a technique that involves cutting, shredding, tearing or punching out a cloth or paper material that will then be used to create a pattern or design picture. Mosaic is high touch but also draws on color and texture to make a rich learning and creative encounter.

Description: Provide materials for the mosaic and a sturdy background on which to create the mosaic. Show children a few examples to help them *bridge* over to this new experience. Use the Mosaic Matrix below to help stimulate your own creative ideas.

Possible Materials	Methods	Adhesives	Possible Backgrounds
tissue paper	punch	colored glue	recycled file folders
wallpaper sample or old greeting cards	tear	white glue	construction paper
construction paper	cut	paste	wood
felt pieces	trace shapes	craft glue	wallpaper samples
wrapping paper	strips	clear glue	fabric

Note: The matrix is meant to be used openly. Skip around and choose one from each list. They are not in a special order. Be creative.

The Personal Touch

Touch is relaxing and creativity enhancing for adults as well. However, we may become so tense and wrapped up in our work or duties, it is easy to neglect our own feelings of creativity. Here are a few ideas for restoring creative feelings in a personal way.

✔ Keep a jar of rose or almond-scented hand lotion on your desk. Take a few minutes to massage some into your hands.

✔ Place a Slinky™ in your drawer. When you are feeling stressed or trying to solve a problem, play with the Slinky™ for a few minutes.

✔ Exercise daily. This is the best creativity enhancer for adults. You release endorphins (natural pain killers) in the brain, and this frees your mind to think, not worry. A walk or bike ride is fine. A swim is great. A game of tennis works, too. The point is to *enjoy the exercise* as much as to do it.

✔ Splurge on a facial, massage or manicure once a month. This kind of rejuvenation is priceless.

✔ Wear comfortable, colorful fabrics. They will help you feel good and thus more creative.

✔ Revisit a childhood hobby that made you feel creative. Buy yourself some nice chalks, watercolors or architectural blocks. Enjoy.

✔ Name yourself as a creative teacher. Think of yourself as that kind of person, and you will find that you more easily adopt those creative postures. Creative persons are not nuts, nor "artsy." They are individuals who embrace life and revel in it. Why not you?

Time . . . the Vitamin That Feeds Creativity

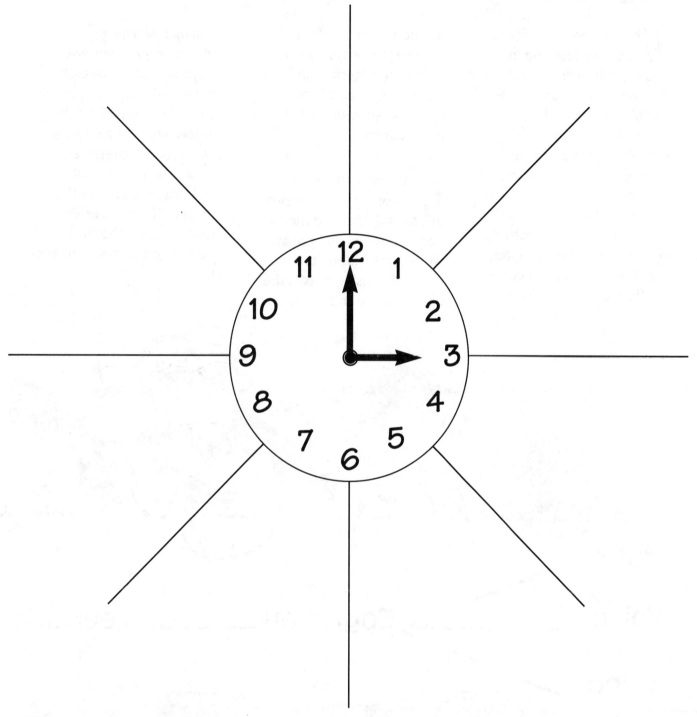

The research on creativity in children suggests that time is the vitamin that feeds creative minds. Children need time for messing around with ideas, manipulating materials, thinking, touching, tearing, drawing, writing, building, painting and making stuff that they can be proud of. We know that, but do we manipulate the classroom clock to allow for that to happen? Use the pretend clock above to brainstorm ideas for carving out chunks of creative time in your classroom. It is your assignment. Let's see how creative you can be, and how committed you are to enhancing creativity, to going beyond hands-on in your classroom.

Chapter 6

Music, Voice and Sound That Go "Beyond Hands-On"

Why include a section on auditory learning in a book devoted to alternative, sensory modalities of teaching and learning? After all, don't we have *enough* lecture and questioning in the classroom? Aren't we talking too much already? The answer to the last question is . . . probably. However this final chapter, like the ones that preceded it, offers unusual, unique methods and insight and unexpected ways to use common materials and ideas as teachers move beyond hands-on in their instruction.

Instead of lecturing and questioning, albeit appropriate and effective methods in a balanced approach, we will talk about techniques for using music, the human voice and sounds to enhance learning. Moreover, we will discuss ways to use these techniques within larger, more social context of teaching in learning. As always, we will connect these techniques to the field of cognitive science and continue to ask: "How does this sense impact the brain and how might it then influence learning?"

Music

Voice ⟶ Cognition ⟶ Learning

Sound

Music, Voice and Sound That Go "Beyond Hands-On"

Professor Myra Jordan, chair of the departments of music and music therapy at Charleston Southern University, has devoted two decades to training music therapists, educators who use music as a healing and teaching tool specifically with the disabled, the sick and the very young. She offers these ideas for using music to enhance learning in the primary classroom:

✔ Learn to play an autoharp. (In a one-day workshop, you can become a musician!)

✔ Use rhythmic chants to teach factual information (number facts, word families, geography facts).

✔ Make up a "rap" to help reinforce facts or concepts.

✔ Pair a chant with corresponding movements (clap, snap, slap knees).

"Two plus three is five"
Clap-snap-clap-snap-clap
or
"AT-Cat; AT Hat; AT Sat"
Clap/clap-slap knee;
clap/clap-slap knee;
clap/clap-slap knee

✔ Use the technique of the Rondo (see page 129) to motivate children.

✔ Invite a music therapist to observe your classroom, and offer specific techniques for individual children. (**Note**: You can include music therapy in a handicapped child's individualized education plan.

✔ Try the hidden sticks game (see page 130).

Professor Jordan enthusiastically supports regular classroom teachers in using music to enhance learning, because "we have only scratched the surface of what music medicine can do." She goes on: "Music reaches children where they are. It is fun and non-threatening. Music not only crosses cultures; it helps children to glory in them!" For additional techniques in music therapy that easily transfer to the regular classroom, teachers might try the "orff-schulwerk" methods, the brainchild of Carl Orff, a German composer and educator. *Schulwerk* means "schoolwork," and this method combines language, movement and music to help young children develop their language, dexterity, rhythm and listening skills through fun, hands-on activities.

Music, Voice and Sound

Though Professor Jordan's ideas embrace a 1980s view of music, there is a fascinating, ancient tradition of using music to influence learning. In the book *Healing Music* by A. Watson and N. Drury, the authors discuss techniques used by the early Greeks. Zithers were played by the

with may cares and concerns? The climate of violence and stress, both in homes and on the streets, has a subtle yet profound impact on young children. We see this manifested in their short attention spans, excessive clingy behaviors and aggressive actions with other children. Perhaps

singing might be a real deterrent to learning. Instead, think of your voice as a real tool, gently probing and pushing the mind, tilling up the soil of thought and the earth of feelings. It is your personal instrument and one that we seldom take time to tune and test.

ancient Greeks as an accompaniment to meals to aid digestion, and according to the Cassidorus, the Aeolian mode of music could be used to treat mental disturbance and induce sleep. The Lydian mode, often considered ideal for children, was intended to 'soothe the sour when oppressed with excessive care.' "

Is there any doubt that today's youngsters often arrive at school burdened

music could be used more effectively to direct their attention, soothe their anxieties and shape their behaviors.

The use of voice, specifically intonation, pitch and timbre on the part of teachers and care givers could easily be enhanced and shaped to become a teaching tool. Have you ever considered your own voice as a teaching tool? I don't mean for singing! If you are like me, your

Finally, simple rhythm instruments, bells, triangles and drums, can be used to create sounds that stimulate the mind. Experts often cite "rhythm" as a critical force in learning, because it has both physical and emotional powers. "Rhythm is a feature of the basic pulsing structure of electrons and a characteristic of our breathing-running-walking patterns, the beat of your hearts and the very structure of speech patterns." (*Healing Music*)

114

Even teachers who have little formal preparation can use rhythm instruments and achieve pleasing, compelling results. Look ahead to page 116 for a list of 10 Sound-Producing "Musts" for the Primary Classroom. How many do you have right now? How might you secure those that you need?

suggests that "The brain transforms sensory messages into conscious perceptions *almost instantly.* Chaotic, collective activity involving millions of neurons seems essential for such rapid recognition." In short, the sensory systems seem to assist the cerebral cortex in creating new patterns or new "mind pictures," and they do it in

With your theme or even specific objectives in mind, work on painting a "big picture." How can you stimulate the senses *generally* to produce responses, reactions and behaviors? Plan ahead for sensory learning. Long-range planning is critical for designing curriculum and instruction of any variety, yet teachers and administrators often neglect to

As you move into the final chapter of this book, you may be thinking . . . "This is complicated" or "It is too much work." That's okay, because that is how our brains perceive all of the sensory experiences that assault it, every waking and sleeping moment, for as long as we live! But here's the clincher, new research

rapid succession, all day long. Some call it a gestalt. We know that out of the choas comes a mind picture that is unique for each child; still the pictures work together, in an amazing, flexible way.

Think of your "beyond hands-on" instruction as creating mind pictures.

set aside adequate time to do it well. Use color, scent, taste, texture and sound within the framework of the planning matrix to create a gestalt in your classroom, a mind picture that puts learning in a fresh, new focus for you and the children that you care about.

10 Sound-Producing "Musts" for the Primary Classroom

1. Bells ... wrist bells, cowbells, bells on a string, hand bells

2. Tambourines (can be homemade)

3. A cassette or CD player (portable)

4. Recordings of music ... classical selections, marching music, dance tunes, nature sounds, jazz, children's songs

5. A set of bongo drums (check yard sales or flea markets)

6. Several pairs of maracas

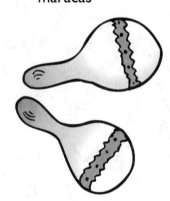

7. A good quality playground whistle

8. A pair of cymbals (I'm not kidding)

9. Two or more telephones (real, if possible)

10. A set of primary grade rhythm instruments (the ideal!)

Creative Connections

Rationale: Soothing, yet stimulating recordings of "natural things" can stimulate children's imaginations or prompt memories of pleasant outdoor experiences.

Technique: After reading a story that contains scenes or characters from nature (whales, swamps, birds, meadows), lower the lights and ask the children to listen quietly as you play a recording of one of the following:

- ✔ sounds of the swamp
- ✔ whale songs
- ✔ sounds of the meadow
- ✔ birds songs
- ✔ ocean sounds

Use this experience to reinforce one or more of these primary grade skills:

- ✔ listening
- ✔ auditory discrimination
- ✔ verbal fluency
- ✔ auditory memory
- ✔ creative thinking
- ✔ problem solving
- ✔ small motor skills (drawing, cutting, pasting)

The next five pages offer some simple, yet creative ways to reinforce learning through the use of sound.

Name _____

Listen to Nature

Directions: After listening to the nature recording, work with your partner or small group to make a list of all the sounds that you heard. Then draw a picture of "what you think" the scene looked like.

Skill: Listening

This is what we heard in the _____ .

_____   _____

_____   _____

_____   _____

_____   _____

This is what I think it looks like in the _____ .

118

Cutter

Finder of Pictures

Sticker

Time Keeper

Directions: After listening to the nature sounds recording, from old magazines cut out pictures of the animals, grass, water or sky that you "heard" in the picture. Imagine what the scene looked like, and then create a collage using the pictures and paste. A collage is a lot of little pictures glued together. Try not to have any white space on your paper. Fill it with color!

Group Size: Cooperative groups of four

Materials: Nature magazines, travel brochures, catalogs, safety scissors, paste, tagboard

Working in a group is an important skill. Use the name tags above for this and other cooperative group activities. Laminate and punch holes to make a "necklace."

Do You Hear What I Hear?

Directions: After listening to the nature recording, look at the list of words or pictures below. If you heard this sound, circle the item in green. If you did not hear this sound, circle the item in red.

Skill: Auditory discrimination, auditory memory

We left an important sound out . . . can you draw a picture of it?

Directions: The telephone is a natural, wonderful prop for the classroom. Use a real phone (unconnected) to encourage fluency? Children should work in pairs for this activity, so you will need two telephones. Guide the children in pretending to "call a friend" and tell him or her about what was "heard" on the nature tape. Children take turns acting as the "caller/teller" and the "listener." After completing the activity, children can cut out and decorate the phone above with nature stickers or natural items such as leaves, nuts or pine straw to reinforce the lesson.

Skill: Creative thinking and small motor

Tell Me a Story

Directions: After listening to the nature recording, you may have a lot of interesting ideas about what was going on. What animal sounds did you hear? Was there water? Do you think it was warm or cool in the place? Use the tape recorder and blank tape to record your ideas. Tell me a story about *what you heard*.

Provide a tape player and blank tapes. The goal is *verbal fluency*; just let the children talk. Use the checklist below if you wish to place an evaluation of this activity in the child's speech and language portfolio. Be sure to date and label the class tapes.

Language Checkpoint

Child: _____   Date: _____

Activity Description: _____

_____

Evaluator: _____   School: _____

Skill	Strength	Competent	Needs Improvement
Length of Sentences			
Syntax and Grammar			
Description/ Creative Use of Language			
Articulation			

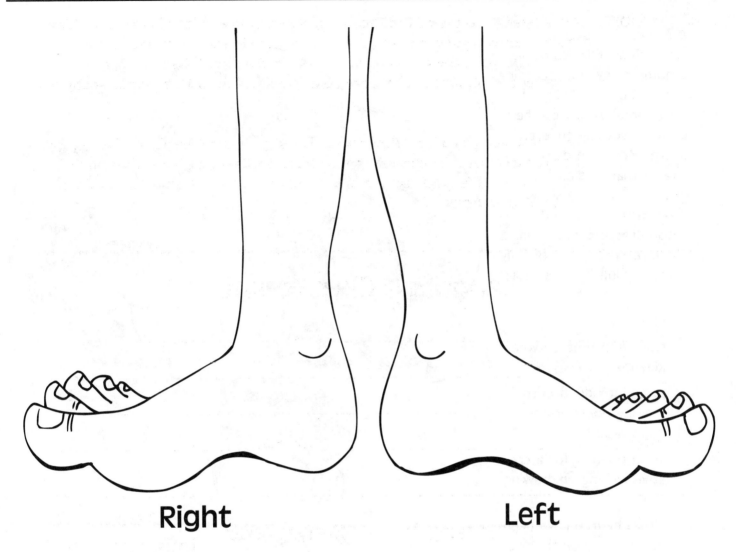

Right   **Left**

Rationale: In the primary school, gross motor activities are always listed on checklists and report cards, yet we often neglect these important skills. Coordination gives children confidence, which boosts their attention span for lots of learning. At least twice each week, put on some marching music, and help children to learn the critical "left and right" skills for both arms and feet! Children can cut out the feet above, and you can use them in a variety of ways.

✔ March in place and practice identifying right and left.

✔ March around the room, and when the music stops, hold up the "left or right" foot on command.

✔ Hold hands, facing a partner and march in place. Try to stay in rhythm.

Lullaby Time

Quiet, reflective music, such as lullabies by Brahms or even a recording of folk music or spiritual "sleeptime" songs, can be useful in settling children down. Research demonstrates that music of this genre can actually slow down heart rates and blood pressure, producing a more relaxed group of children. Try lullaby music for:

✔ rest time

✔ transition time between activities

✔ as an introduction to reading poetry or a story aloud

✔ as an opening for a creative writing or drawing time

✔ after children have been upset, angry or anxious about an event

✔ Take a look at Chapter 3 for ideas using scent, such as lilac, to relax children or ease tension.

✔ Try different kinds of lullabies, tradition, folk songs, spirituals and instrumental music. Encourage children to complete the lullaby thoughts response form on the right.

Three words that tell how this song makes me feel are

_____,

_____ and

_____.

"Why Don't You Use Sound To" Chart

Task	Instruments or Sound Makers to Try			
Signal a Transition	whistle	cymbals	bell	song or tune
Get Children's Attention	maracas	tambourine	beat a drum	clapping
Background for Center Time	nature sounds	classical music	instrumental	
Sound Effects for a Story or Puppet	shake cups of beans/rice	drums	whistle	bells
Teach Counting Skills	beat a drum	triangles	bells	drop marbles on tin pan
Following Directions	marching tunes	Hap Plamer/Raffi/ other teaching tapes		
Auditory Discrimination	bells	triangles	drum beats	tambourine

Make a Tambourine

Whether you call it a tambourine or as my little girls named it, a "shaker," these homemade instruments bring as much joy and learning through the *process* as they do in the *product*! To create these sound makers, select one "holder" from List A and one or more "fillers" from List B. Seal your shakers with an item from List C, and shake, rattle and roll!

List A Holders	List B Fillers	List C Sealers
whipped topping bowls with lids	dried rice, beans or peas— all sizes and colors	masking/duct tape
margarine containers with lids	unpopped popcorn	craft glue
tin pie pans, placed face to face	dried pasta, all sizes and shapes	rubber cement
Styrofoam™ plates, face to face	buttons, bottle caps, milk caps	wax/hot glue
small coffee tins, with lids	marbles	
rectangular, "flavored coffee" tins with lids	sand and pebble mixture	
empty oatmeal or salt boxes with lids		

Singing to Learn

Rationale: The sound of the human voice is powerful and pleasing. For centuries, singing, really a form of recitation, has been a teaching tool. Stimulate learning by creating *original teaching tunes* of your own. Simply insert concepts or vocabulary into familiar children's songs or rhymes.

Directions: Don't expect all or even most of the children to be familiar (at first) with tunes such as "Twinkle, Twinkle"; "The Muffin Man" or songs from cartoons. Start by playing the music and songs from a few simple recordings, and then introduce your innovations. Here is an example.

To the tune of "The Muffin Man"

Do you know the four seasons?
The four seasons, the four seasons.
Do you know the four seasons?
The seasons of the year.

Yes I know the four seasons.
The four seasons, the four seasons.
Yes I know the four seasons.
The seasons of the year.

Summer, winter, spring and fall.
Spring and fall, spring and fall.
Summer, winter, spring and fall.
They come 'round every year.

Extend your lesson with accompanying fingerplay props, such as craft stick puppets, or keep time to the singing with homemade "shakers" on page 126. To encourage cooperation and good listening skills, teach the children to sing the songs in "rounds," or do "boys only," then "girls only." Be sure to print each new "song" on chart paper, and use bold-colored markers to help children recognize new words (see Chapter 2).

Name _____

You Try It

To the tune of "_____"

Your song "_____"

_____

_____

_____

_____

_____

_____

_____

_____

_____

_____

_____

Ideas for Fingerplay Props to Accompany Song

_____

_____

_____

_____

_____

_____

_____

128

The Rondo: A Partcipatory Game with Rhythm

The Rondo is a musical form that fits beautifully with whole language techniques that we use today. In the Rondo, a rhyme is paired with movement to teach a specific skill. The rhyme is chanted by the group, and yet *individual children* get an opportunity to embellish the chant with movements. It looks like this:

A...B...A...C...A...
D...A...E...the pattern continues.
"A," of course, is the rhyme or chant, and the other letters represent individual children.

Here is an example of a Rondo, used to teach the concepts of color and patterns.

1. Children stand or sit in a circle. A basket of colored Unifix™ cubes, in the colors that you are learning, is in the middle of the circle.

2. Children repeat the following rhyme. They may clap and snap in a pattern as well, or not.

    Orange and yellow
    What a lucky fellow
    Orange and yellow
    What a lucky girl
    (or boy)

3. After each repetition of the chant, a new child goes into the circle and puts together a "pattern" of orange and yellow cubes. He or she then instructs the children to "clap and snap" out the pattern.

4. The pattern might be yellow, yellow, orange or orange, orange, orange, yellow.

5. The Rondo can be used to teach words, facts, concepts or rules. Children have an opportunity to be creative and to participate in their own learning. It is a good reinforcer, because it is repetitive and simple.

Hidden Sticks . . . Help You Find Out About Children

Rationale: Auditory discrimination is a skill that young children need in order to learn to read and participate in most lecture and questioning in the classroom. It demands two skills: really careful listening and discernment of sound patterns. Remembering that many of the children we teach today have either experienced frequent early ear infections (see introduction) or have been raised (in part) by television or loud video games, it is no surprise that standardized test scores often reveal serious delays in auditory discrimination and its cohort: auditory memory. Hidden sticks activities help children practice both skills in a fun, nonthreatening way.

Materials: A set of sticks from a rhythm instrument set or a pair of wooden dowels from the craft store and one or more of the following: a drum, a wooden box, a large coffee can or a metal pot (hit sides or bottom).

Procedures: Literally hide the sticks and drum behind a curtain, rocking chair, your desk and beat out rhythms, counts or patterns for children to discern. Make sure that you are not so hidden as to muffle the sound or so far away as to confuse children.

You might:

1. Beat the sticks together in a pattern; then ask the children to clap out the same pattern. Memory.

2. Tap the drum or pot a number of times; then ask the children to tell you how many times you beat it. Counting.

3. Hit three or four different items (box, pan, bell, etc.), and then ask the children to tell you which one you hit first or third. Ordinal numbers.

4. Beat out patterns of varying speed, intensity or rhythm, and then ask children to describe the patterns. (Fast, slow, bouncy, scary, quick, light) Verbal fluency and vocabulary.

5. Give each child (if you have enough) a pair of sticks, or take turns in the group and let them "match" what you did.

The Personal Touch–Your Voice . . . an Instrument

After almost a decade of supervising intern teachers, I can honestly say that "voice" is one of the most critical and neglected tools in good teaching. Experienced teachers learn that a well-modulated, pleasant voice can enhance their teaching tremendously. Yet it is difficult to judge the quality of one's own voice, without some intervention or evaluation. How do you *really* sound to children. Try this personal touch exercise to assess and improve your voice quality.

✔ **Part 1:** Ask a peer teacher or perhaps a parent volunteer or intern teacher to tape a 30-minute audiotape of your lesson. Though video is useful for many purposes, avoid it here. It is too easy to associate your "sound" with gestures or body language. We want to focus exclusively on voice. Select a time when you are *just talking*, not singing. The goal is to evaluate your intonation, volume and timbre during a typical day. Do this on two different occasions to get a baseline.

✔ **Part 2:** Invite an objective third party to evaluate the tape, using the checklist on page 132. Then, before you look at their assessment, listen to the tape yourself, and do the checklist.

✔ **Part 3:** Compare the two checklists. *How many checks do you have in common?* This gives you a fairly decent idea of your voice quality.

Voice Checklist

A

Check each descripton that fits the voice on the tape

- ❑ brash
- ❑ light
- ❑ calm
- ❑ harsh
- ❑ gentle
- ❑ loud
- ❑ melodious
- ❑ grating
- ❑ low-pitched
- ❑ throaty
- ❑ smooth

- ❑ high-pitched
- ❑ whispery
- ❑ heavily accented
- ❑ fast
- ❑ dragging
- ❑ clear
- ❑ garbled
- ❑ thick
- ❑ nasal
- ❑ congested
- ❑ sweet

- ❑ grumpy
- ❑ halting
- ❑ kind
- ❑ happy
- ❑ depressing
- ❑ cheerful
- ❑ angry
- ❑ well modulated
- ❑ evenly toned
- ❑ unevenly toned
- ❑ soft

B

The voice quality was clear and adequately loud.

all the time   most of the time   only at times

The voice projected warmth and caring.

all the time   most of the time   only at times

The voice changed in range to reflect commands clearly but without screaming.

all the time   most of the time   only at times

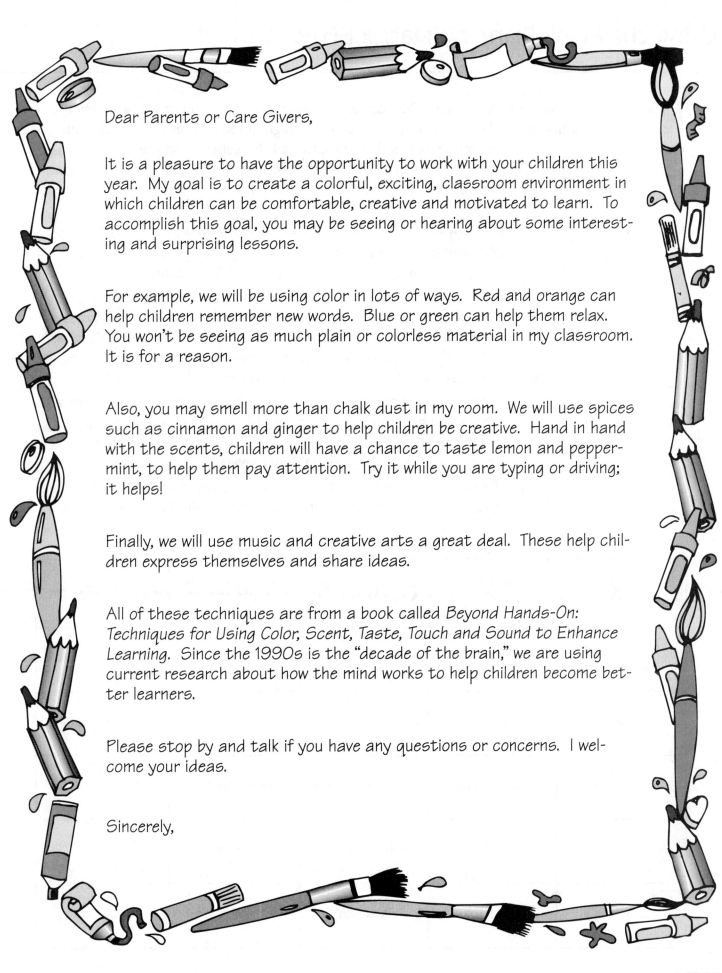

Dear Parents or Care Givers,

It is a pleasure to have the opportunity to work with your children this year. My goal is to create a colorful, exciting, classroom environment in which children can be comfortable, creative and motivated to learn. To accomplish this goal, you may be seeing or hearing about some interesting and surprising lessons.

For example, we will be using color in lots of ways. Red and orange can help children remember new words. Blue or green can help them relax. You won't be seeing as much plain or colorless material in my classroom. It is for a reason.

Also, you may smell more than chalk dust in my room. We will use spices such as cinnamon and ginger to help children be creative. Hand in hand with the scents, children will have a chance to taste lemon and peppermint, to help them pay attention. Try it while you are typing or driving; it helps!

Finally, we will use music and creative arts a great deal. These help children express themselves and share ideas.

All of these techniques are from a book called *Beyond Hands-On: Techniques for Using Color, Scent, Taste, Touch and Sound to Enhance Learning.* Since the 1990s is the "decade of the brain," we are using current research about how the mind works to help children become better learners.

Please stop by and talk if you have any questions or concerns. I welcome your ideas.

Sincerely,

Using the Blank Planning Matrix Effectively

Now that you have travelled "Beyond Hands-On," how can you implement these techniques in an original unit of study? How do you go beyond fragmented tips and fun ideas, and create a unified set of lessons and activities that stimulate all the senses, and therefore learning? Several pages of blank matrices are provided for your convenience. Of course, these can be reproduced and used again and again, and at different grade levels.

Getting Started: ✔ Refresh your memory be reviewing pages 22-24 in the book.

✔ Remember that the matrix is a *planning tool,* not a formal lesson plan. You can develop formal plans from this point.

✔ Resolve to include at least three activities for each of the senses. For example, try to do a "color" activity for oral language, gross motor and social development. On the other hand, you might plan a "scent" activity for fine motor, written language and logic/number. *You need not fill in every box to have a good matrix!*

✔ Revolve your unit around a theme. Choose a theme that is broad enough to accommodate a variety of experiences. The sample matrix on page 24 uses the alphabet. Here are some other themes to try and suggested grade levels.

✔ Recognize that the matrix can be correlated with scope and sequence charts, district curriculum guides and state curriculum frameworks.

4K	5K	Grade 1	Grade 2	Grade 3
Animals and Their Babies	Pets	Living Things	Mammals	Marine Animals
Flowers	Growing Things	Plants	Gardening	Growing Food
My Family	Neighborhoods	Towns/Cities	Using Maps	Continents
Naming Things	ABCs	Words Everywhere	Poems	Stories
Counting	Numbers	Addition	Subtraction	Multiplication

Theme _____   **Grade Level** _____

	Color	Scent	Taste	Touch	Music
Oral Language					
Written Language					
Logic/Number Tasks					
Cross/Fine Motor Tasks					
Social Development					

Theme _____ Grade Level _____

	Color	Scent	Taste	Touch	Music
Oral Language					
Written Language					
Logic/Number Tasks					
Gross/Fine Motor Tasks					
Social Development					

	Color	Scent	Taste	Touch	Music
Oral Language					
Written Language					
Logic/Number Tasks					
Gross/Fine Motor Tasks					
Social Development					

Theme _____ Grade Level _____

	Color	Scent	Taste	Touch	Music
Oral Language					
Written Language					
Logic/Number Tasks					
Gross/Fine Motor Tasks					
Social Development					

Theme _____   Grade Level _____

	Color	Scent	Taste	Touch	Music
Oral Language					
Written Language					
Logic/Number Tasks					
Gross/Fine Motor Tasks					
Social Development					

Theme _____   Grade Level _____

	Color	Scent	Taste	Touch	Music
Oral Language					
Written Language					
Logic/Number Tasks					
Gross/Fine Motor Tasks					
Social Development					

140

Theme _____ **Grade Level** _____

	Color	Scent	Taste	Touch	Music
Oral Language					
Written Language					
Logic/Number Tasks					
Gross/Fine Motor Tasks					
Social Development					

	Color	Scent	Taste	Touch	Music
Oral Language					
Written Language					
Logic/Number Tasks					
Gross/Fine Motor Tasks					
Social Development					

Ackerman, D. *A Natural History of the Senses*. New York: Vintage Books, 1990.

Alschuler, R., and L. Hattwick. *Painting and Personality*. Chicago: University of Chicago Press, 1947.

Arnot, B. "New hope for children with dyslexia." *Good Housekeeping's Family Doctor*. October 1994.

Begley, S. "Gray matters: science shows that men and women use their brains differently." *Newsweek*, March 27, 1995, pages 48-54.

Begley, S. "Thinking looks like this: PET scans show the brain recalling and cogitating." *Newsweek*, November 25, 1991.

Begley, S. "Your Child's Brain." *Newsweek*. February 19, 1996.

Belden, T. "Use of aromatherapy to beat jet lag." *Journal of Commerce*, August 22, 1991.

Birren, F. *Color and Human Response*. New York: Van Nostrand Reinhold, 1978.

Bitcon, C. *Alike and Different: The clinical and educational use of orff-schulwerk*. Santa Ana, California: Rosha Press, 1976.

Blakeslee, S. "Mapping out the human brain." *New York Times*, May 10, 1994.

Bower, B. "Images of intellect: brain scans may colorize intelligence." *Science News*, October 8, 1994, (146), pages 236-237.

Buchman, D. *Herbal Medicine*. New York: Gramercy Publishing, 1979.

Buck, L. "Hue and eye." *New Statesman and Society*, October 18, 1991, (4) 173, pages 29-31.

Dewey, J. *Experience and Education*. New York: Macmillan, 1983.

Diamond, M.C. et al. *The Human Brain Coloring Book*. New York: Harper & Row, 1985.

Edelman, G.M. *Bright Air, Brilliant Fire: On the Matter of the Mind*. New York: Basic Books, 1992.

Eggert, R., and D. Rogahn. "Psychotherapeutic effect of colors." *The Brown Universtiy Long-Term Care Quality Letter*. October 28, 1993, pages 4-6.

Embry, D. "Using color in the 90's as a selling tool." Chain Store Executive. March 1991, page 118.

Freeman, W. "The physiology of perception." *Scientific American*. February 1991, pages 78-85.

Gallagher, W. "How we become what we are." *The Atlantic Monthly*. September 1994, pages 39-55.

Gardner, H. *Creating Minds*. New York: Basic Books, 1993.

Gardner, H. *Frames of Mind*. New York: Basic Books, 1985.

Golden, D., and A. Tsiaras. "Building a better brain." *Life Magazine*. July 1994, Vol. 17, Issue 7, pages 62-70.

Goldstein, M. "Decade of the brain, an agenda for the nineties." *The Western Journal of Medicine*. September 1993, pages 239-241.

Grenfell, J. "Into battle." published in the *London Times*, May 27, 1915. Reprinted in *The Oxford Dictionary of Quotations*, Oxford University Press, 1980.

Appendix

Haas, R. *Eat Smart, Think Smart.* New York: HarperCollins, 1994.

Hammers, M. "Aromatherapy: Soothe yourself." *Vegetarian Times,* February 1995.

Jackson, C. *Color Me Beautiful.* Westminster, Maryland: Ballentine Press, 1987.

Kuppers, H. *Color: Origin, Systems, Uses.* London: Van Nostrand Reinhold Ltd., 1972.

Liberty, M. "Healing oils of aromatherapy." *Better Nutrition for Today's Living,* February 1993.

Livingstone, M. et al. "Physiological and anatomical evidence for a magnocellular defect in developmental dyslexia. Proceedings of the National Academy of Science, September 1991, Vol. 88, pages 7943-47.

Marem, M. "Productivity: The surprising science of workplace effectiveness." *Success,* September 1991, (38) 7, pages 30-36.

McIntyre, A. *The Complete Woman's Herbal.* New York: Henry Holt Company, 1994.

McLaughlin, M. "Will Reggio Emilia change your child's preschool?" *Working Mother,* June 1995.

Nash, G. *Creative Approaches to Child Development with Music, Language, and Movement.* New York: Alfred Publishing Co., 1974.

Osguthorpe, J. D. quoted in: "Study links ear infections, day care." *The News and Courier,* July 16, 1995, Charleston, South Carolina.

Rohm, R. *Positive Personality Profiles.* Atlanta, Georgia: Personality Insights, 1993.

Rossbach, S., and Yun Lin. *Living Color.* New York: Kidansha International, 1994.

Saari, L. "Brain Gain," in *The News and Courier,* August 9, 1995, Charelston, South Carolina.

Schwartz, E. "The changing minds of children: growing up in a context-free reality." *Omni,* January 1995, pages 28-29.

Shannon, J. "Dyslexics need the blues." *Health,* February 1991, page 24.

Shaywitz, S., and B. Schwitz. "Mans' world, woman's world: brain studies point to differences." Science pages of the *New York Times,* February 28, 1995.

Skurka, N. *The New York Times Book of Interior Design and Decoration.* New York: Quadrangal Books, 1976.

Sylwester, R. *A Celebration of Neurons: An Educator's Guide to the Human Brain.* Alexandria, Virginia: Association of Supervision and Curriculum Development, 1995.

Watson, A., and N. Drury. *Healing Music: The Harmonic Path to Inner Wholeness.* Bridgeport, England: Prism Press, 1978.

White, J. "Color: The newest tool for technical communicators." *Technical Communication.* August 1991, (38) 3, pages 346-352.